THE MODERN GUIDE TO
VINTAGE JEWELLERY

THE MODERN GUIDE TO
VINTAGE
JEWELLERY

Beth Bernstein

ACC ART BOOKS

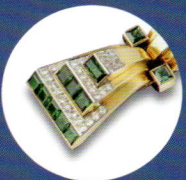

I became acquainted with vintage jewellery as a young girl. From the age of 10, I learned about popular pieces through my mother's and grandmother's jewellery, as well as the styles worn in the old movies on TV and pieces I saw friends and family wear while growing up.

My maternal grandmother, Ida, was a jewellery enthusiast and savvy shopper; she scored her real pieces scouring second-hand shops and travelling abroad. Early in my adolescence, she would create a glamorous world for me when I went to stay with her in Brooklyn, New York. She would let me stay up way past my bedtime and pour ginger ale into her best champagne glasses as she laid her favourite real and faux styles out on her nightstand for both of us to wear while watching the late, late movies on TV. I dressed up in her clip brooches – some in my hair and others affixed to the collars of my pyjama top – while she fastened around my wrist her prized possession: a wide Art Deco bracelet, set with onyx and coral. I styled colourful 1950s cocktail rings on multiple fingers on each hand. The films

we watched ranged from the late 1930s through the '60s and included jewellery from some of the most renowned Houses at the time. I was too young to recognise the brands until later on when I became a jewellery editor and journalist, but I knew that the pieces she collected were similar to the pieces we saw in the films.

I was mesmerised by jewels worn by the style-setting actresses in their iconic roles: the pieces owned and donned by Norma Shearer, Joan Crawford and Paulette Goddard in the 1939 film *The Women* by designers such as Trabert & Hoeffer-Mauboussin and Raymond Yard; the faux clips Bette Davis wore in *All About Eve* (designed by Hollywood legend Joseff), the jewels Marlene Dietrich wore in *Stage Fright* and *Desire* (Van Cleef & Arpels and Trabert & Hoeffer-Mauboussin, respectively); and the pinky ring, starburst brooch and diamond necklace worn by Katharine Hepburn in *Holiday* (by Fulco di Verdura for Paul Flato and Paul Flato). I was at my grandmother's the first time I ever saw the melodramas of the 1950s and early '60s: Lana Turner in *Madame X* and Susan Hayward in *Backstreet*, both in pieces designed by David Webb. The styles that Hayward wore were reported

< Unusually large cushion-cut aquamarine with three baguette diamonds on each shoulder. Mounted in a platinum cathedral setting with a scroll motif in the gallery and split prongs. American, circa 1950. Courtesy of A La Vieille Russie

<V Natural pearl and diamond double-clip brooch that can be worn as a brooch or two separate clips, by Marcus & Co., circa 1930s. © Sotheby's

> Katharine Hepburn wearing jewels by the House of Paul Flato in a still from the 1938 film *Holiday*. © Columbia Pictures/Diltz/Bridgeman Images

V Lana Turner wearing a David Webb turquoise suite in a still from the 1966 film *Madame X*. © Dilitz/Bridgeman Images

to have sold out the day after the film opened. These jewels, worn throughout the 20th century in films, set the style for women everywhere and still influence jewellery collectors today.

Like many women of the era, my mother wore a charm bracelet; she would add new charms with each milestone she celebrated in her life. I remember hearing the clanging and jangling on her wrist as she prepared meals or picked me up from school. The charms represented her life as a young girl, daughter, wife and mother. As I played with and examined each charm, I was particularly attracted to the moveable styles that my grandmother gave her from the '40s. My mom, who was a natural beauty – a mix

of Natalie Wood and Jackie Kennedy – worked as a runway model to put herself through acting school, which she then quit after marrying my father. She had sublime taste. During the early to mid-'60s, she travelled to London to purchase her clothes at Mary Quant, Biba, and on Carnaby Street and the King's Road. I remember when I was about 6 years old, propping myself up on her dressing table and watching her get ready for a night out with my father. I still recall certain pieces he gifted her: a floral diamond Van Cleef & Arpels Mystery Set brooch, Tiffany & Co. pearls, and the famed Schlumberger gold and enamel bangle, just like those that Jackie Kennedy wore.

By the late '60s/early '70s, she changed her style to reflect the changing times. This was the era of Watergate and the peace rallies for the Vietnam War, calling for a pared down, less opulent, less flashy approach to fashion and jewellery. My mother received her original Aldo Cipullo 'Love' bracelet in 1970, just a year after they came out, and just two years before my parents' divorce. She handed it down to me when I was in my 20s and I haven't taken it off since. My mother went back to work during the second-wave feminist movement, which continued from the '60s into the '70s. She switched her jewellery to the more organic, sculptural pieces of Elsa Peretti and Paloma Picasso for Tiffany & Co.

I became obsessed with the Elsa Peretti bone cuff and open heart pendant, and was ecstatic when I received them for my 16th birthday. During the '70s disco era, I would dance the night away, with my fake ID, under flashing neon lights with a yellow gold omega choker, a variety of different size and style hoop earrings, and my bone cuff on one wrist and the 'Love' bracelet on my other.

In the years to follow, after working as fashion writer, photo stylist for magazines and wardrobe stylist for TV, I launched a new career as a jewellery journalist. While writing an article about buying jewellery at auction, I interviewed Simon Teakle, who headed up the US Jewelry Department of Christie's for 20 years before opening his own shop in Greenwich, Connecticut. While I was sitting in his office at Christie's, he brought in some of the major pieces that were to be in the Magnificent Jewels sale that season, and placed an iconic Cartier 'Tutti Frutti' bracelet from the 1930s around my wrist. Throughout the interview, I couldn't stop marvelling at its construction, the beauty of the carved gemstones, and how light it felt wearing it.

Over the last 22 years in my role as a jewellery journalist and editor, I have come to realise that vintage jewellery represents the cultural landscape of three generations of my own family, as well as groundbreaking global innovations and the ability of some of the most renowned Houses to change with the times and continue to bejewel international collectors.

I hope you will be captivated and delighted by the jewellery throughout the book and perhaps be lucky enough to start or add to your collection, renewing a part of the history of the 20th century and keeping it alive for future generations.

The Modernes
Late 1920s—1935

Le Corbusier, recognised as the 'father of modern architecture' and a good friend of leading jeweller Jean Fouquet, said at the time: "To be modern is not a fashion, it is a state. It is necessary to understand history, and he who understands history knows how to find continuity between that which was, that which is, and that which will be."

The changes that took place from 1920 to 1935 in art, architecture and fashion, as well as the new modern lifestyle, drove the pulse of the Art Deco movement, inspiring jewellery design at the time. Sandwiched between two wars, the movement was a tour-de-force of inventive pieces that spread across Europe to the United States with the speed of travel. The jewellers were trailblazers, ushering in a new sense of freedom and artistic expression. The first part of the period, during the early '20s, took a revolutionary approach, rejecting the ornate flowing forms of Art Nouveau and, instead, focusing on shapes that were three dimensional and geometric. This was also the age of transatlantic travel, commercial passenger flights, and, in defiance of the economic downturn, the hedonistic Jazz Age. Chanel's sporty chic and elegant classics took Paris by storm and then crossed the Atlantic. Hemlines were up, necklaces plunged to the navel, waistlines were low, spirits were high and speakeasies and the right to vote offered women new-found freedoms. Across the United States and Europe, women smoked, bobbed their hair and enjoyed everything from leisure activities to dancing the night away.

Cubism and Futurism were taking over contemporary art. Architecture and interiors were streamlined, strong and imposing, as seen in the iconic Chrysler Building in New York City. Traditional, ornate jewellery was replaced with striking and innovative styles. The linear and angular elements of the new architecture and art were reinterpreted as shapes and motifs in significant and popular pieces. The jewellers of the day were pioneers, ushering in a new sense of freedom and artistic expression. As with each period or movement, rather than remaining static, the proponents evolved their styles to create some of the most inspirational jewels of the 20th century.

The Exposition International des Arts Décoratifs et Industriels Modernes showcased all manner of decorative arts, architecture and design in Paris in 1925, and highlighted the Style Moderne. (But it wasn't until 1966 that the movement

< A pair of Mauboussin 'Tutti Frutti' double clips with carved rubies and sapphires, kite-shaped and baguette-, round- and square-cut diamonds, mounted in platinum, French, circa 1925. Courtesy of Sandra Cronan
∨ Enamel, moonstone, diamond and onyx bracelet by Cartier, circa 1925. Courtesy of Pat Saling Jewelry Collection

became known as Art Deco.) Among the many renowned jewellers represented at the Expo was Jean Fouquet, a founding member of the Union des Artistes Modernes, which was committed to promoting this new innovative style. The jewellery of this era, produced a century ago, continues to entice and enchant collectors.

An early proponent of Art Deco was French jewellery designer Raymond Templier. Heavily influenced by Cubism, he produced some of the boldest pieces of his day, contrasting opposing arcs with semicircles, utilising inverted triangles, and playing with volume as well as geometry. Like many other Houses of the time, he produced jewellery in rock crystal, platinum and diamonds.

As Art Deco evolved, it increasingly looked to Asian, Middle Eastern and African cultures, with a special focus on Egypt after Tutankhamun's tomb was

opened in 1922. Jewellery Maisons such as Cartier, Van Cleef & Arpels, Boucheron, Georges and Jean Fouquet, Mauboussin, Chaumet and La Cloche, all embraced these influences, absorbing motifs and symbols and adding a bold splash of colour to the previously monochrome Art Deco aesthetic. During the 1920s, Cartier in particular led the way, taking inspiration in colour and texture from India's popular carved gemstones, artfully cut into stylised flowers, leaves and plants, which came to be referred to as 'Tutti Frutti' (fruit salad). Persian and Islamic art and colour combinations also influenced Cartier during this time. The House reinterpreted them with an unabashedly innovative style, contrasting bright diamonds with vibrant rubies and

> Bracelet showcasing the transition to the more streamlined Art Moderne style of the 1930s, featuring emerald-, baguette- and round-cut diamonds, mounted in platinum, by Cartier, circa 1930. Courtesy of Lee Siegelson

sapphires with onyx and black enamel. This vivid look would influence other important brands.

As time went on, carved jade, coral, onyx and natural pearls from China and Japan were integrated into the designs in the form of pagodas, stylised flowers, dragons and other orientalist motifs.

When the Wall Street Crash and Great Depression of 1929 hit, the exuberance of the vibrant colour mixes of the Roaring Twenties was toned down again. Jewellery pieces were still bold and glamorous, yet revealed a return to an all-white platinum and diamond aesthetic.

Despite the severe downturn in the economy, as Pat Saling of Pat Saling Designs in New York City explains: "The wealthy were still wealthy and still desired shining examples of the great Houses of the day." Custom designs were ordered and Hollywood's Silver Screen actresses wore the jewels coming out of France. Cartier was a master at evolving and moving with the times, as displayed by the rock crystal, diamond and platinum bracelets made in 1930 and sold to Gloria Swanson. She can be seen wearing them in two films: *Perfect Understanding* in 1932 and the famed *Sunset Boulevard* in 1950.

Lee Siegelson of New York City, who has owned and sold some of the most iconic jewels of different time periods, explains: "The later Art Deco period, particularly in the 1930s, represented a shift from the bold, geometric designs of early Deco towards a more refined, streamlined aesthetic. This period saw jewellery embracing softer, more fluid lines, as well as a focus on symmetry and form. The materials remained luxurious, but the designs reflected the changing tastes of a society leaning towards elegance and subtlety."

Technological advances in diamond cutting resulted in stunning combinations of a variety of geometrically shaped diamonds: baguette, emerald, princess cuts/square French cuts, half moons, trapeze shapes and marquise, which fitted together like a modern mosaic in bracelets

their own take on the feeling that was spreading across Europe and the USA."

The 'Tutti Frutti' style was bold and was recaptured in all its glory in the necklace Cartier designed in 1936 for style arbiter and heiress to the Singer sewing machine fortune, Daisy Fellowes, who was a dedicated customer of the House. Two magnificent 'Tutti Frutti' bracelets were custom designed during this same time period for Linda Lee Porter, Cole Porter's wife.

During this period there were also advancements in settings that were indicative of the Maison in which they were

that range from medium to ultra-wide, clip brooches and on-the-lobe earrings.

In the mid '30s, colour returned to French jewellery in a substantial way, infusing it with what were considered unorthodox combinations of cabochons, carved hardstones and different cuts of diamonds. This imbued the jewellery with dimension, while the colours offered a more exotic feel thanks to the use of rubies, sapphires and emeralds, coral and jade, mixed with hardstones such as lapis lazuli, malachite and onyx. Says Saling, "The Indian Mughal and other cultural influences didn't end with the Great Depression – the style resurfaced but with different elements added and refined as each renowned brand created

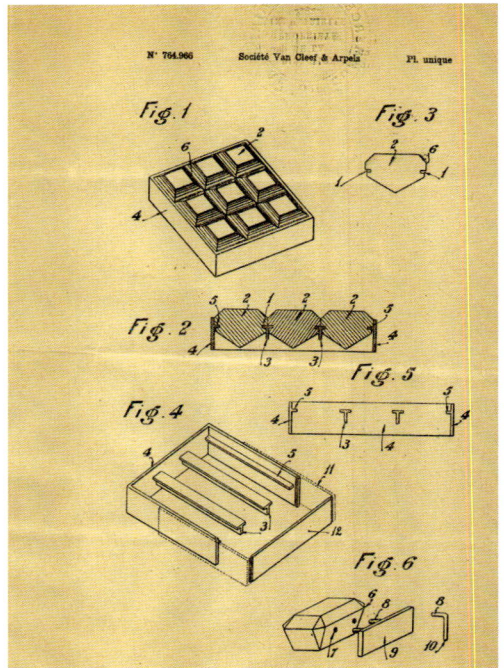

> Raymond Yard Art Deco double-clip brooch, set with round- and baguette-cut diamonds, mounted in platinum. It can be worn as a brooch or separately as clips. Signed "Yard". American, circa 1930. Courtesy of Sandra Cronan

made. Van Cleef & Arpels's Mystery Set was perhaps the most ingenious of the time, developed and patented in 1933. These invisible mountings allowed the jewel to have uninterrupted surfaces from which they could combine a whole design of coloured calibrated gemstones. The Van Cleef & Arpels Mystery Set continued into the 20th century in a variety of motifs and styles of jewellery and is a mainstay of the renowned Maison.

Jeanne Toussaint took a novel approach to the latter part of the Art Deco period and brought in yellow gold to designs that had, until this point, been predominately platinum set. These pieces were set in inventive combinations of semi-precious stones, such as amethyst and aquamarine, with precious gems and hardstones that enlivened Cartier's palette and created yet another landmark in Cartier's design lexicon.

Popular Styles

Clip brooches or dress clips

The clip brooch was a savvy multifunctional design, constructed as one large brooch with a mechanism in the back that allowed it to be detached and worn as two separate clips. They were worn throughout the Art Deco period, pinned to the straps of gowns, to large wraps and stoles, or to either side of the neckline of a dress. They were also used to accessorise shoes, bags or hats. Many of the Deco clips were set in platinum with different cuts of white diamonds, but as demand for them grew, they were set with other precious gems, most often with rubies and sapphires. Sandra Cronan notes: "They were a jewel that many American stars wore on film, adding to their popularity." Today, they still feel current when collectors wear them, either in the same ways as originally intended or as hair ornaments, attached to the collar of a jacket or the bottom of jacket sleeves. They have also been one of the jewels of choice on male celebrities at red-carpet events – one of the 'man brooches' that have been enjoying popularity over the past five or so years.

Clip-on / on-the-lobe earrings

Cronan reports: "The elegant linear earrings, drops and chandeliers of the '20s moved to shorter, bolder clip earrings during the 1930s." Women grew out their garçonne look and short bobs that had dominated the Roaring Twenties

< Diamond sautoir approximately 38cm long, featuring two stylised greyhounds on the detachable pendant, French, circa 1925. © Sotheby's
> Geometric 'Pagoda' on-lobe dangle earrings with transitional-cut diamonds set in platinum, circa 1935. Courtesy of Platt Boutique Jewelry
>∨ Bracelet with calibré rubies and round-, baguette- and French-cut diamonds set in platinum by Drayson, London, late 1930s. Courtesy of A La Vieille Russie
∨∨ Cartier gem-set, diamond and enamel 'Tutti Frutti' bracelet. © Sotheby's

and the designers of the day met the new styles of shoulder-length wavy locks with earrings that made a statement by combining different cuts of stone and sat on the lobe, which complimented both short and longer necklaces.

Flexible bracelets

Bold yet easy to wear, another style in vogue throughout the entire Art Deco period was the flexible bracelet, which incorporated intricate piercing work in all-white platinum settings with an arrangement of different cuts of diamonds. Baguettes, marquises, rounds, half moons and early emerald cuts were surrounded by smaller diamonds in sophisticated compositions in medium to ultra-wide styles. Some were geometric with additional details such as buckle closures, but most lay flat on the wrist. Delicate, stylised floral patterns comprised of rubies and emeralds, highlighted with lacquer or enamel, were set against a background of gleaming diamonds, creating a painterly feel. Precious gemstones and semi-precious stones of amethyst and aquamarine were

set in between the diamond patterns, while carved and cut sapphires, rubies and emeralds were set in the 'Tutti Frutti' style of the Art Deco period.

Sautoir necklaces

Ultra-long sautoirs, popular throughout the Art Deco period, were often designed in all-white colourways, featuring

geometric diamond and platinum pendants at the bottom of a long diamond and platinum chain. Some examples included tassels of beads that could be knotted nonchalantly and worn down the front or back of a dress. Often these tassels swung from circular rings or enamelled, carved pendants on silk cords. They took on cross-cultural influences before and after the Great Depression, with inspirations coming from China and India, which introduced carved jade, coral and onyx pendants.

Multi-purpose jewels

It was perhaps after the Wall Street Crash and the Great Depression that designers became really savvy about creating multi-functional jewels. Sandra Cronan says: "These jewels that could be broken up and worn differently were ultra popular in the Georgian era creating an imaginative way to allow one jewel to function as many. The designers of the Art Deco period ran with this concept, creating mechanisms that really allowed for pieces to be worn in multiple ways." For example, Cronan has

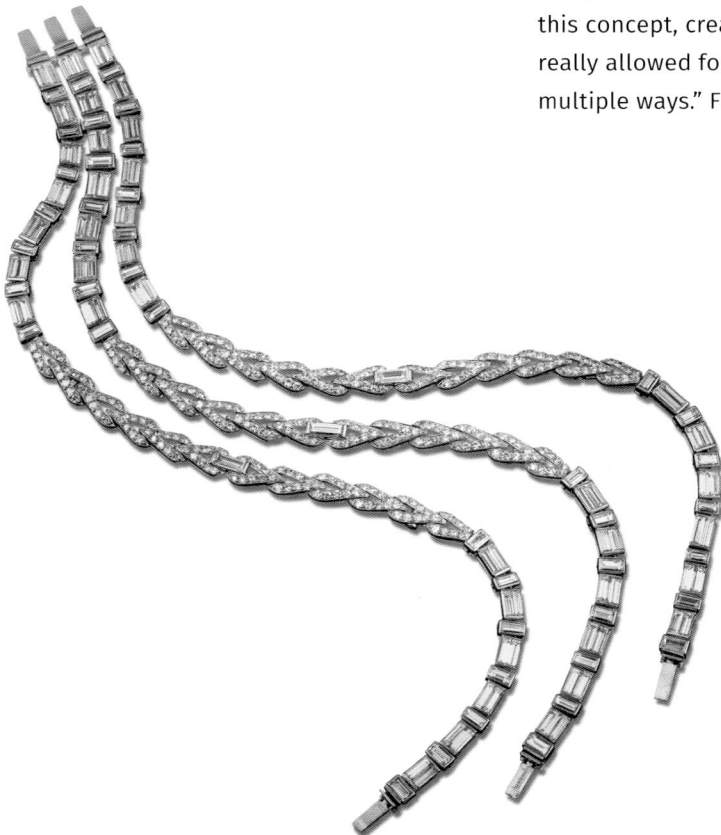

> Sapphire and diamond double-clips bracelet by Cartier.
© Sotheby's

V Art Deco black onyx, coral and diamond bandeau,
French. Courtesy of Simon Teakle

in her collection three bracelets that can clasp into a long necklace. "You can also attach two of the bracelets in a choker and wear it with the third bracelet as a matching set," she explains.

Clip brooches were also designed with cuff bracelets; each clip could attach to the open front on either side of the bracelet for a chic and elegant look.

Necklaces and earrings featured detachable drops that could be added to different styles of brooches.

Bandeaus, one of the most popular hair jewels during this period, were designed in platinum and gemstones. These were low profile and usually worn across the forehead with a ribbon tied at the back of the head, offering a more youthful and less formal alternative to tiaras. They would sometimes be designed to be separated into bracelets or worn as chokers. If you are lucky enough to find a bandeau designed to act as both a hairpiece and a choker, and possibly split up into bracelets as well, then you have scored one of the most coveted, adaptable jewels of this time period.

The Feminine Touch
Women Designers

In the years between the two world wars, irrepressible and groundbreaking female jewellers tore down the gender boundaries and made an indelible mark in what was, ironically, a male-dominated industry.

For much of time, it had been men who created the pieces that each generation of women wore and who dictated the jewellery styles that would become a popular reference for each period recorded in time. Of course, there were certain women of nobility whose choice of jewels set the style during their reign. Think of Queen Victoria, whose young marriage to Prince Albert produced the Romantic period of jewels that she wore, as well as the mourning jewels she donned for 30 years after his death, which influenced trends throughout Europe. And her daughter-in-law Queen Alexandra was responsible for elegant dog collars and chokers coming into favour during King Edward VII's short reign. From her marriage to Napoleon III in 1853 onwards, Empress Eugénie (the last Empress of France) established the style for jewellery worn in France and also throughout Europe – a dazzling array of diamond floral designs, crescent moons, stars and bows. Yet, for all these women, it was true that their jewels were still crafted, designed and executed by men.

How refreshing then for the women designers who landed on the scene in the 20th century. With their own compelling and daring aesthetic that differentiated them from what had come before, they created a new style that would be seen as modern and wearable for years to come.

Coco Chanel, Jeanne Toussaint and Jeanne Boivin – who hired both Suzanne Belperron and Juliette Moutard – were pioneers, who rivalled their male counterparts with styles that were revolutionary. As women, they understood

what would appeal aesthetically to female customers, move well and feel comfortable when worn, and was infused with a sense of luxury and personal expression. They forged new ground and changed the way we look and wear jewellery today, making it possible for the women jewellers who followed them to take their rightful place in jewellery's history.

Jeanne Boivin

The well-known House René Boivin, a favourite of English aristocracy, was founded in 1890. René's wife, Jeanne, was sister to the famed fashion designer Paul Poiret, who invited them to parties and dinners and introduced them to the fashionable set of the upper classes of the day. When René passed away in 1917, Jeanne Boivin completed her husband's existing orders and, by doing so, became the first woman ever to take the reins and direct a French jewellery House.

Jeanne was neither a trained designer nor jeweller, but had gained a wealth of knowledge from her husband. She also had ideas of her own and drew inspiration from her friends, such as the writer Collette and dancer and singer Josephine Baker. A savvy business woman, she decided to hire two female designers, mentoring them while allowing them to develop their own talents. Suzanne Belperron and Juliette Moutard had very different styles, but both conveyed in their designs what was happening during the 1920s–40s in Paris. They brought the modernity to jewellery that Jeanne foresaw for the House; visionary pieces that were comfortable to wear and feminine, yet radically distinctive in innovation and technique.

Germaine Boivin joined her mother as a designer at the House in 1938, and she continued to run the company after her mother's death in 1959. The House of Boivin changed hands a few times before

being purchased in 1991 by the Asprey Group, which closed the business shortly afterwards. Despite this, Boivin remains a major influence in the history of jewellery and a testament to the artistic vision of the women who created some of the most arresting designs of the times.

Suzanne Belperron

When researching my book *Jewelry's Shining Stars: The Next Generation; 45 Women Designers* (ACC Art Books), Suzanne Belperron was cited by many of the contemporary artists as most influential in their careers. This didn't surprise me, as Belperron was a prolific, wildly imaginative talent, who was ahead of her time. She mixed precious and non-precious materials, creating her own definition of fine jewellery and what it meant to her. Her fashionable clients included, but were not limited to, Elsa Schiaparelli, the Duchess of

Windsor and Diana Vreeland. Her designs represented a world of character and style rather than status. One of the great tastemakers of the 20th century, pioneering a new sensibility in jewellery, she never signed her work, stating: "My style is my signature". Born Suzanne Vuillerme on 26 September 1900 in the town of Saint-Claude, her family moved a year later to Besançon, which was home to the first public museum in France and birthplace of the national watch industry. Her mother saw talent in her daughter, enrolling her in the École des Beaux-Arts in Besançon, from which Suzanne graduated with a portfolio of drawings and paintings that were the first peek into her utterly unique and pioneering design aesthetic. After settling in Paris, she took more classes and met Jeanne Boivin's daughter, Germain, which led to her being hired as a modelmaker and draughtswoman by the House of René Boivin at the age of 19. Jeanne Boivin recognised Belperron's sensibility and use of materials, and realised that she designed in a way that other jewellers had not yet explored. While at Boivin, Belperron pioneered setting precious stones in semi-precious material. In 1924, at 23 years old, she became co-director of the House of

Boivin. Later in her career, Belperron became known for her affinity to the raw texture and buttery colour of 22K gold, which she called "Virgin Gold". Due to the softness of 22K, her workshop developed the technique of backing and reinforcing it with 18K and then hammering, chiselling or burnishing the gold to achieve the antique patina that Belperron desired.

Pat Saling, an expert and collector of Belperron pieces, explains: "Belperron was more of a jewellery sculptor than a designer, so ahead of her time and

◄ Sapphire, diamond, platinum and grey-gold Bib necklace, by Suzanne Belperron for Herz-Belperron, 1946–55. © Belperron

► Diamond, platinum and grey-gold 'Spiral' earclips/ brooches, a convertible system, by Suzanne Belperron for B. Herz, 1932–40. © Belperron

creating pieces so different than what everyone else was doing. I think part of being young is that you don't realize how unique you are or that you are a visionary." Saling continues: "She worked with a lapidary who understood her imagination and made her vision come to life. If there weren't tools that could carve the stones, they would invent them for her designs, from a ring carved out of a single block of chalcedony to the floral hardstones set with precious gems, just a few instances that were avant-garde for the times. She also understood how the pieces would sit or move on a woman's earlobe or wrist, that the pieces needed to undulate with curves and contours, which I believe separated her from her male counterparts."

By 1932, Belperron was ready to leave Boivin and branched out to work with Paris's renowned stone dealer Bernard Herz. The company flourished. Without a store to sell from, Belperron would go to see customers in their private offices; she hit her stride, winning many celebrity clients as customers, including The Duke and Duchess of Windsor. After the outbreak of WWII, both Herz and Belperron were arrested by the Nazi regime. As she wasn't Jewish, Belperron was allowed to go. Herz asked her to purchase and rename the company Suzanne Belperron, S.A.R.L. in order to keep the business going during the Nazi occupation of Paris. Belperron tried but could not secure Bernard Herz's release and he did not survive the war. However, his son Jean did survive. On Jean Herz's arrival back in Paris, Belperron offered the company back to him, to which he responded by making her an equal partner. The House of Herz-Belperron remained in business until Suzanne Belperron's retirement in 1974.

During her career, Belperron's work often appeared in contemporary magazines. In the *Binghamton Press*, June, 1951, journalist Rosette Hargrove

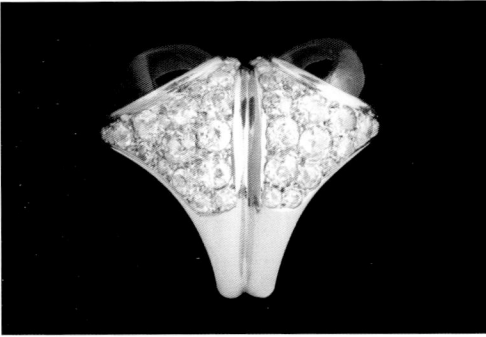

wrote: "Suzanne is unorthodox in her designing methods. She has been known, for instance to sink a 15-ct marquise diamond into a scooped out ring of rock crystal. Or to use hundreds of round and baguette diamonds to create glittering veins in crystal and thus produce clips and a matching bracelet." In 1961, the *San Francisco Chronicle* wrote: "Spotting her jewels is a favorite sport practiced at such fashionable occasions as theater first nights or charity balls. Clues to recognition include an abstract fluidity of form, a Pharaonic or Aztec sheen that gives a centuries-old patina and a highly personal technique of setting precious gems in larger semi-precious stones. The final quality that causes Belperron fans to build up a complete collection of her jewels is that every one is personalized to the owner...

The moulding of a jewel to personality is guided by the experience of years. The unwritten Belperron rules are subtle and secret. But as an example, she reveals that since few faces are perfectly symmetrical, pendant earrings should rarely be the same size!"

It was the 1987 Sotheby's auction in Geneva of The Duchess of Windsor's jewels that led dealers and collectors alike to be fascinated with the jewels of Belperron once again. Only five out of 16 pieces were correctly catalogued as Belperron jewels. It was reported that this was likely due to the fact that Belperron did not sign her pieces and many had been custom-made for The Duchess of Windsor. However, Belperron's entire body of work was finally recognised and sold at high value.

In 1998, Ward Landrigan, owner of Verdura, purchased the exclusive world rights to her archive of 9,200 designs. During his former post as head of the US jewellery division at the renowned auction house Sotheby's, he had been

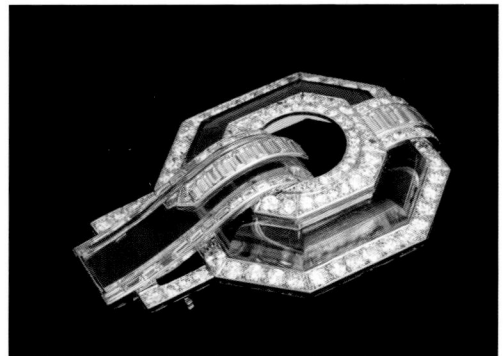

> 'Bague Quatre Plans', platinum and diamond ring, by Juliette Moutard for René Boivin, France, 1933. Courtesy of Fred Leighton

passionate about her work. When, in 2012, Suzanne Belperron's personal jewellery collection came up at auction in Geneva, Landrigan acquired 22 of the lots for the Belperron Museum Collection. Today, Nico Landrigan, Ward's son and President of Verdura, is responsible for the revival of Belperron's work, which continues to reach new collectors who admire her spirit and her profound influence on jewellery throughout the 20th century.

Some of the most popular pieces from her career include her 1930s double-clip brooches in carved rock crystal set with diamonds, rings carved from various hardstones with gemstone accents, large floral motifs – such as flower heads and leaves carved from chalcedony – and other gem materials on their own or as the clasp of multi-strand beaded necklaces. She favoured circular, sculptural or geometric motifs, including spirals, shells and fans. Perhaps her most iconic designs were her carved-stone bangles.

Juliette Moutard

Another pioneer of her time, Juliette Moutard was hired in 1933 by the House of Boivin, where she remained for the rest of her career until her retirement in 1970.

Paris-born, Moutard gained degrees from two Parisian art schools.

As the Boivin house designer, Moutard remained very much behind the scenes, with most of her creations being either unsigned or signed simply "R. Boivin" for the House. In time, Jeanne Boivin and Juliette Moutard moved on from the Art Deco aesthetic to more naturalistic and sensual, rounded forms in a vivid combination of shapes, textures and coloured gemstones.

At first, Jeanne Boivin and Juliette Moutard's designs continued to echo those that Suzanne Belperron had produced whilst at Boivin. But, with time, they branched out to create jewels that remained representative of the House, yet were distinctive and innovative and that the bohemian elite, celebrities and socialites, such as Daisy Fellowes and Claudette Colbert, coveted and found alluring. Jeanne Boivin and Juliette Moutard worked in harmony together and, by the mid- to late 1930s, Moutard's originality and ingenuity were at the forefront of the House's designs.

◀ Cabochon and carved-amethyst necklace and bracelet interspersed with chrysoprase beads in 18K gold, designed by Juliette Moutard for René Boivin, Paris, circa 1950. Courtesy of A La Vieille Russie
▼ Amethyst and emerald ring, House of René Boivin after a drawing by Juliette Moutard, France, circa 1947. © Sotheby's

Boivin never had a storefront, nor they did advertise; their private viewings were by appointment only and they designed mostly commission work. Moutard's passion was botany, which took shape in her floral and foliate designs. She also had an imaginative flair with birds and animals and an affinity for starfish and sea life, all of which were rendered in colourful gemstones; fish scales were designed with a flexibility that became a speciality of the House. Eventually, she turned to tactile trims and fabric for inspiration, bringing three-dimensional bows and tassels to her jewellery designs.

Lee Siegelson described Juliette Moutard as: "one of the driving forces behind René Boivin's innovative designs from the 1930s to the 1970s. She had a knack for combining bold, avant-garde elements with a refined elegance. Her work is known for its daring use of texture and form, setting a new standard for jewellery that wasn't afraid to break away from traditional norms. She brought a unique vision to Boivin, making pieces that were wearable but still had that artistic flair." He continues: "Her designs often featured nature-inspired motifs, but she reinterpreted them in a modern way, using materials and techniques that were ahead of her time. Moutard's ability to infuse movement and dimension into her work made her a standout designer in mid-century jewellery. She played a huge role in shaping the aesthetic of the House during her time there, but she remained pretty low-profile, which is why not as much is known about her compared to her contemporaries."

Juliette Moutard's 'Starfish' Brooch

One of the most recognisable and brilliant jewels that Juliette Moutard created was the 'Starfish' brooch. Initially designed in 1935, it was a painterly colourful masterpiece and featured in both *Vogue* and *Harper's Bazaar*. In 1938, it was purchased by the actress Claudette Colbert, best known for her Oscar-winning role in *It Happened One Night*. The 'Starfish' passed through several owners before being purchased by Lee Siegelson, who, 80 years after it was designed, sold it to the Museum of Fine Arts, Boston, where it resides today in the permanent collection. MFA curator, Emily Stoehrer, explains the piece's ingenious design: "The simple elegance of the 'Starfish' brooch conceals complex construction that combines form and function. At four inches long, it is roughly the size of an outstretched palm and features 71 collet-set rubies and 665 pavé-set amethysts. Drawn from the *Asterias vulgaris*, a common sea star native to the North Atlantic, the brooch has dozens of sophisticated joints that allow movement in three directions (up and down, side to side, and around). The legs flex and drape with the same wave-like motion as the marine creature it represents. Initially designed in 1935, the 'Starfish' took years to perfect. In 1938, while travelling in Paris, American actress Claudette Colbert purchased the brooch. Even if she had seen the brooch illustrated in *Vogue* (1937) or photographed in *Harper's Bazaar* (1938), it would have done little to prepare her for its sensual nature. Colbert had a lifelong love of the ocean, so it's easy to imagine her delight when she was presented with the brooch at Boivin's atelier on Avenue de l'Opera."

Juliette Moutard's ruby, amethyst and gold 'Starfish' brooch, made by Charles Profilet for René Boivin, France, 1937. © Museum of Fine Arts, Boston © Bridgeman Images

Coco Chanel

When we think of Coco Chanel, we get an instant image of a designer who changed the perceptions of personal style. Nothing about her own style or the jewellery or clothes that Chanel designed was traditional. It was all a play on convention, from freeing women of bodices and corsets, to inventing casual dress. Throughout the '20s, she wore multi-strands of faux pearls, with a strand or two of real ones mixed in, haphazardly, with costume and fine gold chains. She once proclaimed: "A woman needs ropes and ropes of pearls."

Put simply, Coco Chanel changed the course of fashion and, with it, achieved a rapid rise to fame. After moving from Deauville in Normandy, her small atelier in Paris had grown to an entire building by the early 1920s. Coco Chanel dictated trends and developed tips and quips on jewellery and fashion, for which she became well known. In 1930, Chanel hired Fulco di Verdura to assist her in creating a jewellery collection. He designed the Maltese cross theme, which was perhaps Chanel's most iconic jewellery: the motif appears in pendants and brooches and the multi-coloured precious and semi-precious gems set into gold and bold enamelled cuffs on the wrists of the most style-setting women throughout history.

Chanel continued to influence generations, and images of her have become part of our collective consciousness. In 1932, in what would seem a paradoxical move for someone known for the simplicity of her creations, Chanel presented her first fine diamond jewellery collection. These creations were inspired by her lover, French illustrator and designer Paul Iribe. Iribe was not the only influence: the effects of the Great Depression could be seen in all areas of life, including fashion, but Chanel pushed back against the drabness of bleak austerity. Breaking with tradition and with the techniques of formal jewellery design, she accepted a commission from the International Diamond Guild to help boost sales. Working with some of her favourite motifs, Chanel presented the Bijoux de Diamants exhibition – a

◀ Coco Chanel's diamond 'Fountain Fall' necklace and 'Shooting Star' ornament/diadem displayed on a mannequin at the original Bijoux de Diamants exhibition, 1932. © Albert Harlingue/Roger Viollet via Getty Images
▽ Verdura and Coco Chanel in Chanel's studio, on the rue Cambon in Paris, 1937. © Boris Lipnitzki/Roger-Viollet

dazzlingly lavish collection, a galaxy of constellations: shooting stars, crescent moons and comets, all set with melee diamonds, offering the twinkling lights found in the evening sky, presented against her signature chic black.

In the early 1980s, Karl Lagerfeld took over as creative director of the House of Chanel. In 1993, the fine jewellery collection was re-launched with many of the original pieces being brought back into fashion, with new pieces inspired by the originals being added each year. In 2012, to celebrate the 80th anniversary of Coco Chanel's original Bijoux de Diamants exhibition, Chanel debuted a new fine jewellery collection in homage to the original, aptly named The 1932 Collection. And the legacy continues today with new collectors clamouring for the original pieces as well as the modern-day reinterpretations.

Jeanne Toussaint

Louis Cartier's lover Jeanne Toussaint, was a design powerhouse, who had started as a handbag and leather goods designer at Cartier and was considered a barometer of style. Louis Cartier promoted her to the role of Director of Haute Joaillerie in 1933, a position that she continued to hold, even after Louis's death in 1942, until her retirement in 1968. She, too, broke with tradition, and her influences produced some of the Cartier's most iconic pieces, rivalling the most prolific male designers of the time. She sought to free women from the conformity of fine jewellery and looked to the stylistic fashions of the day, always considering what she believed woman would want to wear. During her tenure at Cartier, she created many multi-dimensional, imaginative and, often irreverent, pieces – mixing unexpected gemstones and inspiration derived from animals and plants during a time when pieces were more rigid and geometric. Louis Cartier playfully nicknamed her *La Panthère* (The Cat) as she was the driving force behind the legendary Cartier Panthère collection of stylistic, jewel-encrusted panthers and tigers, which are still being produced today; vintage and new pieces alike are to be seen ferociously stepping out in different forms on A-list celebrities at contemporary red-carpet events.

Toussaint's prowess and instincts about jewellery and what women wanted was instrumental in the Cartier cats becoming synonymous with wearers projecting an aura of confidence and fearlessness. The Duchess of Windsor was a huge fan. The first 'Panther' created for her was in gold and surmounted an

< The Duchess of Windsor's colourful flamingo brooch, by Jeanne Toussaint for Cartier, France, 1940. © Uber Bolder/Alamy Stock Photo

<V The Duchess of Windsor's clip brooch, a three-dimensional platinum panther set with diamonds, sapphires and yellow diamonds crouching on a 152.35-carat Kashmir sapphire cabochon, by Jeanne Toussaint for Cartier, France, 1949. © Shutterstock

V The Duke of Windsor with his wife, Wallis, who is wearing her flamingo brooch. © World History Archive/Alamy Stock Photo

emerald cabochon. Toussaint's design mastery of the Cartier cats developed alongside new techniques, which produced a three-dimensional platinum panther atop a 152.35-carat Kashmir sapphire cabochon, which The Duke and Duchess of Windsor purchased in 1949 in Paris. (Cartier bought back the brooch for its own collection in 1987.) Toussaint was also responsible for The Duchess of Windsor's vibrantly colourful flamingo brooch. She was a proponent of the

Indian influences of the later part of the Art Deco movement and reintroduced Cartier's earlier 'Tutti Frutti' styles with a renewed exoticism for customers such as Daisy Fellowes and other famous socialites. Toussaint continued to innovate and inspire some of the most popular jewellery of the renowned House.

The legacy of these groundbreaking women continues as their jewels pop up at auction, in the collections of renowned vintage dealers, and in the heritage collections often shown in exhibitions. These women pioneered change and influenced the individualistic, confident and bold way we continue to view, wear and purchase jewellery.

Retro Active
1936—1945

∨ Yellow gold, sapphire and diamond buckle bracelet with lozenge links, signed "Tiffany & Co.", circa 1940s. Courtesy of Fred Leighton
> Joan Crawford posing in her stunning Raymond C. Yard citrine suite. © Everett/Shutterstock

Coinciding with pre-war, WWII and the post-war years, the Retro period, from the late 1930s to the early 1950s, witnessed major changes in fine jewellery. It was a dramatic change from the glamorous styles that had appeared as the USA and Europe came out of the Great Depression in the mid-1930s and the latter part of the Art Deco movement.

Germany's invasion of Poland in 1939 initiated WWII and the ravages of wartime took hold across Europe from 1939 to 1945. Two years later, in 1941, the USA got into the war after Japan bombed Pearl Harbor. Across Europe and the USA, young men marched into battle, while women, previously homemakers, took jobs in factories to support the war effort. From the Nazi invasions to the bombing of Pearl Harbor and Hiroshima, it was an horrific time in history. Millions died; countries were torn apart. People throughout the world mustered up the strength to move from the grief and the ravages of the war into rebuilding and resilience.

It's almost too difficult to talk about jewellery from such a harsh time in our history, but jewellery, like art and architecture, continues to be a part of the cultural landscape of the past and the present.

Pre-War

From 1935 to 1937, at the end of the Art Deco movement, jewellers explored new takes on nature-inspired forms and created pieces we now classify as 'statement' jewellery. "These pre-war years focused on engineering: pieces

< Van Cleef & Arpels 'Tubogas' gold necklace, circa 1940. Courtesy of MS Rau
∨ 18K gold 'Gas Pipe' bracelet, French, 1940s. Courtesy of A La Vieille Russie

were bigger and bolder, but designers developed techniques so that no piece felt too heavy to wear," says Adam Patrick, manager of A La Vieille Russie in New York City. Benjamin Macklowe, President of Macklowe Gallery, describes pre-war jewellery as "becoming more voluminous, rigid, and weighty. Retro jewellery continued to incorporate geometric motifs from Art Deco but added a third dimension to them, departing from the linear and two-dimensional platinum jewellery of the Deco era and embraced boldness over delicacy".

Jewels were designed to give the appearance of being heavy even when they were not. Popular styles included convertible pieces, Ludo designs by Van Cleef & Arpels, fish-scale links, calibré-cut stones and the innovative flexible Tubogas necklaces and bracelets – these all remained popular through to the postwar years. Tubogas, which translates literally to 'gas pipe' in Italian, is created from a pair of interlocking gold strips wrapped tightly together to form a flexible and hollow tubular length that does not need to be soldered. Initially used industrially, it first made its jewellery debut during pre-WWII times.

This technique was utilised and made famous in Bulgari's Serpenti designs, which became popular again in the late 1960s and '70s.

War Years

Jewellery makers faced multiple challenges due to wartime constraints. As the main issue was getting hold of raw materials, the industry transitioned into reworking materials supplied by customers. Although gold became the primary material, the trade of gold was banned in France; clients had to provide their own to jewellers, with the Banque de France deducting 20% of the melt value. Platinum, which had been used extensively in most Art Deco jewellery,

> Voluminous and angular 'Tri-colour' bracelet with 18K yellow and rose gold horseshoe-shaped links joined by white gold arches, Vicenza, Italy, circa 1938–44. Courtesy of the Macklowe Gallery
V Machine aesthetic 18K gold ring set with sapphires and diamonds, by Henri Lavabre, Paris, circa 1940. Courtesy of A La Vieille Russie
V> Emerald-cut brandy citrine clip earrings, mounted in 18K gold, fans with diamond tips, English, circa 1940. Courtesy of Sandra Cronan

was banned for making jewellery during the war due to it becoming essential for military use. To create variety, instead of using 18K gold, resourceful jewellers used 10K and 14K gold mixed with various alloys to feature different colours – rose, yellow and green-gold – often in a single piece.

As women took on different roles, such as working in factories while the men were away fighting, jewellery design became more austere. This austerity turned into a bolder, yet innovative take on three-dimensional utilitarian styling and wartime themes, with necklaces and bracelets

influenced by strong shapes designed in the 'machine age' aesthetic.

To counter the scarcity of precious gems during wartime, there was a move to setting semi-precious stones, such as aquamarine, topaz and citrine, for use as large centre stones as well as accents. Throughout the Retro period, yellow gold continued to be the predominant material in jewellery. The lack of access to the usual metals and gemstones once afforded to jewellers in peacetime, challenged them to invent new techniques and to work with alternative materials, leading to a creative outpouring of motifs and silhouettes ranging from geometric to naturalistic styles.

The Popular Pieces

Starting during the transition from Art Deco to Retro in pre-war times, convertible styles became the jewels to own: from necklaces that turned into bracelets, to pendants that detached to form earrings. This was not the first time transformable jewellery was popularised – it dates back to antique times – but we find more curvy lines, asymmetry and volume in the Retro creations. (And it would not be the last, this multi-functional approach to jewellery would be seen again – in the 1950s, through the '70s, and then again in the 21st century.)

Brooches that split into two clips, which emerged in the Art Deco period (see Chapter 1), continued to be worn both ways, but with gemstones or diamonds set into gold rather than platinum, and often in swirling shapes that evoked fabric trims, which we also see again, post-war.

"**Bold, semi-precious stones**, including aquamarine, topaz, citrine and amethyst, replaced precious gems as the latter became scarce in Europe," says Macklowe. This can be seen in the jewels of the legendary collector Joan Crawford. In addition to her huge collection of large sapphire pieces, which earned her the nickname 'Joan Blue', she was a poster celebrity for the swirling statement jewellery set with large semi-precious stones, often designed for her by Raymond Yard (see Chapter 4).

Jewellers would also use **synthetic rubies and sapphires** instead of real gems, and set huge semi-precious stones into rings and necklace centrepieces.

Van Cleef & Arpels's Ludo motifs and Mystery Set pieces, which the Maison had developed before the war, continued to reign throughout the Retro period.

> 18K gold oval clip set with sapphires and diamonds, American, circa 1940. Courtesy of A La Vieille Russie
∨ 18K gold tank-track, concave-link bracelet, Italian, circa 1945. Courtesy of A La Vieille Russie

Wartime influences on jewellery took shape in perhaps the most quintessential styles of the mid-Retro period. The inspiration came from tanks on the battlefield and treads from factories, featuring step-like sections of bracelets, which were bold, ultra-wide, three-dimensional and brilliantly constructed, but never too hefty to wear. These were simply called **tank and tread bracelets**. They were developed in single tone, two-tone and tri-tone golds, and were flexible and comfortable to wear. Out of many of the war-year Retro pieces, they are the most coveted today.

Hidden watches and belt bracelets were also pieces that were significant during this period.

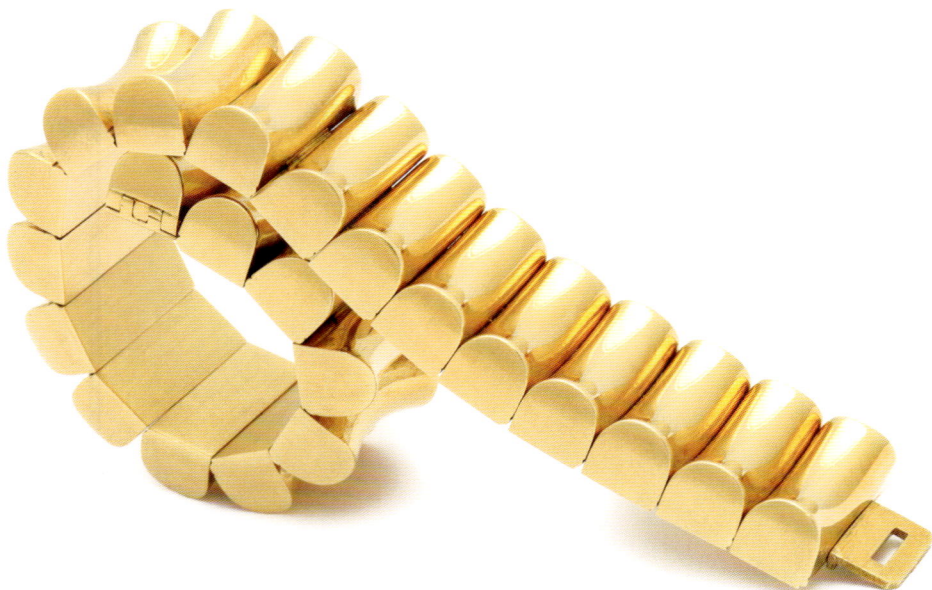

< 'V for Victory' money clip with gemstones set as three dots and a dash, representing the letter "V" (for victory) in morse code. Gifted to Mr. Kriendler, co-owner of the famed 21 Club in New York City, dated 1941. Courtesy of Circa 1700
> 'Flower' clip, 1936. Platinum, yellow gold, Mystery Set rubies, diamonds. Van Cleef & Arpels Collection.
© Van Cleef & Arpels SA.

Emblematic designs became another prevalent theme at the major Houses. Cartier's famous 1942 'Caged Bird' brooch in the colours of the French flag, symbolising occupied France, was on prominent display in the Maison's rue de la Paix shop window. Then, two years later in 1944, Cartier developed another brooch, representing the Liberation, with a bird at an open door of a cage.

Van Cleef & Arpels, Boucheron, and Mauboussin all crafted **patriotic pieces** during this time. As the war neared an end, a niche market of 'Liberation' jewellery popped up. These patriotic jewels were crafted in the form of military symbols of freedom, such as flags and eagles. This jewellery was all made in gold and adorned with brightly coloured, vibrant stones of red, white and blue.' World War II Allied 'V for Victory' jewellery was also extremely popular.

Charms also became representative of the period, such as sentimental sweetheart charms (which were designed to remember loved ones far away) and military insignias, which featured all branches of the service, from sailors and anchors to fighter planes and wings, to name just a few. The US Liberty Bell was another charm that spoke to patriotic motifs. Three-dimensional and moveable **mechanical charms** also dangled from women's wrists starting in the 1940s and then continuing into the postwar '50s (see Chapter 6).

Patrick comments on a shift in tastes in the late 1940s: "People wanted to wear more vibrant hues and were influenced by cultures far and wide. The influences and aesthetics start to really blend in the Retro years from 1938 onward to other periods in jewellery." He continues: "It's important to remember that the predominant looks don't just stop and end at each decade. Style is fluid, designers adapt and their ideas crossover and evolve into the next era. Classic pieces such as diamonds set in platinum remain popular decade over decade. That being said, it's really apparent that the most exceptional pieces from those times were made of gold."

The jewellers of the Retro period created bold futuristic looks with limited resources at accessible prices. The designs played with weight and scale, shaping metals to be larger and rounded and more three-dimensional along with the enthusiastic use of coloured stones.

The post-war years featured a more fluid, yet still bold, approach with animal and floral motifs, as well as textile-inspired designs, including bows, knots, ribbons and tassels, which continued into the '50s.

Peter Schaffer, co-owner of A La Vieille Russie, notes: "Although each period has its unique charm, the styles of Retro work with the widest range of modern fashion trends for any time of day. This aspect is alluring to a new generation of jewellery enthusiasts and provide strong, impactful pieces for today's collectors."

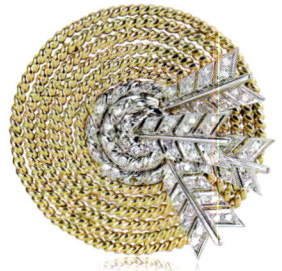

< Cartier convertible 'Night and Day' diamond brooch, circa 1945. The petals rotate to transform from plain gold to diamond-encrusted, allowing the wearer to transition their jewellery seamlessly from day to evening wear. Courtesy of MS Rau

<V Pair of gold, diamond and platinum 'Target' brooches, 1940. Originally from the collection of Mrs. William Paley (later Dorothy Hirshon). © Verdura

> Yellow gold, emerald and diamond ring, signed "Boucheron, Paris", French, circa 1940s. Courtesy of Fred Leighton

V 18K gold triangular 'Tubogas' bracelet with bombé-peaked links, bound by three stepped bands star-set with old single-cut diamond accents, French, circa 1940s. Courtesy of the Macklowe Gallery

Macklowe concurs, and adds: "A visually striking appearance and ease of wear has led to the renewed popularity of Retro jewellery among collectors. Yellow gold, a prevalent material in these pieces, seamlessly integrates into daily attire, allowing for versatile dressing options. This adaptability sets it apart from other times in jewellery. As a result, we've seen an increase in prices, especially for sought-after styles like tank bracelets." He concludes: "The prices of Retro jewellery can vary widely depending on factors such as the rarity of the design, the quality of materials, and the presence of significant motifs. While the use of less-expensive materials during the war years may have initially influenced prices, the growing demand for Retro jewellery has contributed to its appreciation in value."

Star Power
Film Stars and Jewellery Houses

After having watched so many films curled up in front of my grandmother's television in her Brooklyn apartment, and soaking in the style of many of the leading ladies of the cinema, I couldn't help but devote a chapter to the jewels and renowned Houses these actresses and movies introduced me to, as well as The Duchess of Windsor, Jackie Kennedy and Diana Vreeland to name just a few whose personal style and stories behind their jewels have influenced women around the world.

From the mid-20th century onwards, celebrity sightings rather than royal style dictated the jewels bought and sold internationally. From the 1930s through the 1960s, stars of the silver screen and international socialites influenced popular jewellery tastes on film and in magazines, and wherever women could get a glimpse of these style setters who could afford anything they desired. But it was Hollywood's Golden Age that had the most impact, with film icons being regarded almost like nobility. So when Hollywood publications such as *Photoplay* reported that the stars were wearing their own precious gems in films, it gave an even greater allure, with women wanting to emulate the screen sirens.

The Maisons, which designed personal pieces for these iconic women of the period between the 1930s and 1960s, also provided the jewellery for major films, whether they were modern-day, period films, those that helped define the era in which they were made, or showed us a glimpse into the future. Jewels not only supported character development but helped turn the Maisons themselves into household names, building sales and boosting clientele.

Early Hollywood set the bar high, working closely with the powerhouses of Cartier, Tiffany & Co., Van Cleef & Arpels, Paul Flato and Verdura, and later on David Webb and Bulgari. But the trend of lending jewellery to be worn in movies began in the 1930s with **Trabert & Hoeffer-Mauboussin** (T&HM), which was the first House to receive an on-screen credit in *The Gilded Lily* (1935). Then a few years later, the Star of Burma, an 83-carat cabochon-cut star ruby owned by Hoeffer, appeared in the opening credits of *Walter Wanger's Vogues of 1938*. A gloved hand with the magnificent ruby set in a platinum and diamond bracelet opens a curtain with the company's name. The film was shot in Technicolor, making it the perfect vehicle to promote coloured gems and, thereby, the brand.

Trabert & Hoeffer Inc. was initially founded in 1926. Located on Fifth Avenue in New York City since 1930, the company's partners were Randolf J. Trabert and (William) Howard Hoeffer. The partners already had a few years' experience in the jewellery industry before the launch. Though Randolf Trabert died in 1930, Trabert & Hoeffer continued and a shop was opened on Wilshire Blvd. in Los Angeles. Howard Hoeffer's passion for jewels urged him to purchase large exotic stones. In 1936, Trabert & Hoeffer Inc. announced its merger with Mauboussin, Paris, creating Trabert & Hoeffer-Mauboussin.

Known for designing oversized original pieces with large, coloured gems, the jewellery House supplied more and more films. This in turn led to the big stars of the 1930s and '40s wanting their own Trabert & Hoeffer-Mauboussin pieces. The company introduced a wholesale collection, called Reflections, in the early '40s. Eventually the business was dissolved in 1953.

Paulette Goddard's love for all that sparkles was well known. She first wore her Trabert & Hoeffer-Mauboussin diamond-fringed necklace, which could be converted into two separate bracelets, in publicity stills and then in the historical movie *Kitty* (1945), which was set in 18th-century London. It did not matter to Goddard that the necklace was 20th-century-through-1930s style, or that it was out of place with the costumes. She made it work for her.

After Goddard missed out on the role of Scarlett O'Hara in *Gone with the Wind*, her then husband Charlie Chaplin gave her a beautiful ultra-wide gold bangle with cabochon-emerald floral motifs combined with diamonds, plus coordinating emerald and diamond flower clips. She wore the bracelet in many films, including *The Women* (1939). She pinned her earrings to her blouses and dresses and wore them in more unconventional ways, for instance attached as brooches to her Victorian gown in *An Ideal Husband* (1947), once again ignoring the historical period.

The most stylish professional jewel thief in film history has to be **Marlene Dietrich** as 'Madeleine de Beaupre' in the 1936 crime-comedy *Desire*. Dietrich wears her own Trabert & Hoeffer-Mauboussin bracelet with a large emerald and diamonds. She also wore the bracelet in the film *Angel*. In real life, she paired the bracelet with another large cabochon-emerald bracelet from Paul Flato. In

Maria Riva's biography of her mother, she recalls the emeralds, "the largest the size of a Grade A egg and the smallest, no smaller than a large marble".

Paul Flato, also a jeweller to the stars, was best known for his witty designs and his elaborate pieces that were bold yet feminine, mainly designed in platinum. He began his career as a watch salesman in New York in the early 1920s, but soon after opened his own jewellery business on 57th Street in Manhattan. He opened his second shop in Beverly Hills in 1937, by which time he boasted a roster of well-known socialites and film icons as his clients, such as Marlene Dietrich. His pieces were seen on leading actresses in numerous films.

A favourite film of mine, *Holiday* (1938), stars **Katharine Hepburn** as a millionaire's daughter. In it, she wears Flato jewels, including a diamond pinky ring (which would be equally on trend today), a starburst brooch of canary diamonds, and a three-strand diamond collet necklace.

Flato hit hard times. After serving 16 months for fraud, in 1945 he moved to Mexico and lived there for almost eight years. In 1953, he returned to the USA, before going back to Mexico. In 1970, he opened a jewellery shop in Mexico City and spent two decades there, before finally coming back to Texas in 1990. He was one of the American greats whose

and three of them just happened to be William Powell's leading ladies: two in real life and one on screen. Myrna Loy, who acted with him in 14 films, including the *Thin Man* series, owned an important star sapphire, set into a platinum-leaf mounting with baguette diamonds on the shank. According to the ring's most recent owner, Hollywood jeweller to the stars and collector Neil Lane, **Myrna Loy** wore the sapphire in *The Thin Man* publicity shots. Lane notes that this particular Art Deco style is truly reflective of the Golden Age of Hollywood. It is thought the ring was created by Paul Flato.

Powell bought his second wife, actress **Carole Lombard**, a star sapphire ring when they married in 1931. Though they stayed together for just 26 months, the pair remained friends and continued to star in movies together, including *My Man Godfrey* in 1936. Lombard opted to wear her own jewellery in the film, including the huge sapphire ring that Powell had bought for her and a 150-carat sapphire, which she purchased and had mounted as a brooch; it could be converted to be worn either as a ring or a pendant. In the film, she wears the brooch at the neckline of a full-length evening gown with a duster.

early jewels are legendary and ahead of their time. Notably, two designers who worked for Flato went on to become renowned for their own famed jewels: George W. Headley and Fulco di Verdura.

Worn by Hollywood's leading actresses of the 1930s, such as **Myrna Loy**, **Carol Lombard**, **Jean Harlow** and **Joan Crawford**, cabochons sapphires spread across Hollywood, reflecting the extravagance of the Golden Age. They have become increasingly popular again over the past several years among vintage jewellery aficionados, reminiscent of that early 20th century 'sapphire craze'.

The actresses of the heyday of Hollywood wore star-sapphire or sapphire-cabochon engagement rings

There was a story doing the rounds in Hollywood that when leading man William Powell first proposed to **Jean Harlow** in 1936, he offered her a beautiful, but traditional, diamond ring; Harlow accepted the proposal but refused the ring. The platinum-blonde bombshell supposedly felt that a large star sapphire would better suit her personal style. Powell purchased one. Newspapers and gossip columns talked about her wearing it on the set of the comedy *Libeled Lady*, never taking it off, and speculated about whether she and Powell were really engaged. Harlow was still wearing the ring while filming *Saratoga* in 1937, when she was taken seriously ill, and died with Powell at her side.

Joan Crawford was renowned for her love of the gemstone – so much so that the press dubbed her 'Joan Blue'. Through a succession of four marriages and three divorces, Crawford received gifts of fine jewels, and also purchased pieces for herself. She often attached clips to necklaces or wore them attached to head wraps, as well as wearing large gemstone necklaces.

One of Crawford's favourite jewellers was **Raymond C. Yard**, who originally worked for Marcus & Co. He launched his own company in 1922 to serve New York's elite. His jewellery during the Art Deco period was streamlined yet bold, using large coloured stones set in both platinum and yellow gold. Yard was recognised for his attention to detail and involvement in every aspect of design, from sketch to finished product. His work was distinguished by the finest gemstones and pearls, and a subdued elegance that displayed a keen eye for detail and appreciation of the materials, while reflecting the styles of the times.

Yard's straight-line bracelets in platinum, with extraordinarily detailed piercing work and gemstones, characterised his designs during the Art Deco period, while his jewels during, and immediately after, World War II showcased his ability to scout out the best combinations of yellow gold and beautifully cut semi-precious gems.

He had a very discreet, exclusive clientele of socialites and, in the late '30s, after beginning to work her way into becoming one of Hollywood's top-earning and successful stars, Crawford also worked her way onto Yard's select roster. Crawford's first marriage to Douglas Fairbanks Jr – whose father had lavished Mary Pickford with some of the finest sapphires in the world – ended in divorce in 1933. When Crawford became engaged to actor and frequent co-star Franchot Tone, Yard created an engagement ring featuring a 70-carat star sapphire. She already owned a 72-carat emerald-cut sapphire ring, and would often wear them together. The most publicised Yard piece in Crawford's collection was a wide, platinum, Art Deco bracelet featuring fine piercing work with baguette-, half-moon- and marquise-shaped diamonds and three star sapphires of 73.15 carats, 63.61 carats, and 57.65 carats.

Joan Crawford also wore her own jewels in the film *The Women* (1939). The cuff is her Raymond C. Yard jewel with two gigantic half-moon shaped citrines set in a circle. It was part of a stunning suite that included a necklace with a

350-carat citrine and earclips that sold on 5 December 2012 at Sotheby's in New York for $56,250.

Van Cleef & Arpels designed jewels throughout the entire 20th century, creating some of the most intricately detailed and technically advanced pieces that were as beautiful as they were revolutionary. The Maison designed for socialites, nobility and Hollywood royalty. Both from jewellery merchant families, Estelle Arpels and Alfred Van Cleef married in 1895. In 1906, Alfred and his brother-in-law Charles Arpels founded the Maison of Van Cleef & Arpels on Paris's renowned Place Vendôme. Estelle's

brothers Charles and Julien became partners with Alfred, and her brother Louis joined the company in 1912. In 1926, Alfred's daughter Renée Puissant became the Maison's Artistic Director. Her vivid imagination offered a design concept that equalled the unparalleled gems. Soon René-Sim Lacaze joined the Maison as a designer, and together they created a style that blended elegance with whimsy, fantasy, romance and an attention to detail that imbued each piece with the highest standards of quality.

In 1932 and 1936 respectively, the second generation joined the company: Claude and Jacques, followed by Pierre, the youngest, in 1944. One of the spectacular designs of this period was the three-dimensional Jarretière cuff bracelet designed for **Marlene Dietrich** around 1937, which she then wore on screen in the 1950 Hitchcock film, *Stage Fright*. In the film, Dietrich plays 'Charlotte Inwood', a manipulative star of musicals, who convinces her lover to murder her husband. The bracelet features a large loop motif set with cushion-cut rubies; the reverse of the loop is a paved-set diamond floral motif, accented with baguette-cut diamonds. The articulated band of the cuff is set with round-cut and more baguette-cut diamonds. Made

from 73 rubies and 141 diamonds – the bracelet was one of Dietrich's most cherished pieces and is now considered a masterpiece of 1930s design. Dietrich's version of the cuff was more oversized and had more flowing lines than that, say, of the Van Cleef & Arpels Jarretière bracelet of sapphires and diamonds that The Duke of Windsor gave to Wallis on their marriage.

In later life, Dietrich sold off some of her jewels to help her out in difficult situations – such as to pay for back taxes in 1987. When she passed away five years later, her grandson Peter Riva observed that the Jarretière bracelet was the only piece of jewellery she kept. Although it was her favourite piece, after she wore it in *Stage Fright* she kept it locked away in a vault. In 1992, the bracelet sold for far in excess of the estimate at Sotheby's New York and went to a private collector for $990,000, and more recently, in 2023, at Christie's for $4.5 million.

One of the most renowned designers of on-screen jewels during the Golden Age of cinema was **Joseff of Hollywood**, which was founded by young designer and entrepreneur Eugene Joseff in 1928. He was known in studio circles simply as 'Joseff' and publicly as 'Jeweller to the Stars'. He designed and created thousands of realistic-looking costume jewels that made film stars sparkle on screen. His creations can be seen in films such as *Gone With the Wind, Gentlemen Prefer Blondes, Around The World In 80 Days, Cleopatra, High Society, All About Eve* and a host of other famous titles. Stars who wore Joseff's pieces on screen also began commissioning him to create ever more elaborate pieces for them to wear off-screen. American women would see photos of their favourite stars in magazines wearing his jewels and covet them. Around 1937, due to the demand from regular women wanting to wear his jewellery, Joseff expanded his business to retail; the line was sold at Nordstrom, Neiman Marcus, Bullock's, Macy's, and Saks. In one of the most famous scenes in *All About Eve*, Bette Davis is wearing a costume-diamond brooch on a black dress, when she exclaims, "Fasten your seat belts, it's going to be a bumpy night". In a publicity still for *All About Eve*, Bette Davis posed in one of her costumes from the film, including the Joseff of Hollywood simulated diamond brooch.

Another Hollywood jeweller, American-born **William Ruser** was best known for his figurative jewellery from the 1950s and '60s. After serving in World War II, Ruser and his wife moved to Los Angeles and soon opened a boutique on Rodeo Drive. Many stars wore his jewellery on screen and off. Several pieces of **Elizabeth Taylor's** jewellery collection auctioned by Christie's in 2012 were by Ruser.

Duke Fulco di Verdura – a groundbreaking designer whose work was popular throughout almost all of the 20th century – got his start working for some of the most renowned fashion and jewellery Houses. As well as socialising with celebrities and royalty, he designed the jewellery that stars owned and wore on film. Born into Sicilian aristocracy, he was introduced to Coco Chanel by his friends Cole and Linda Porter at a party in Venice in 1925. She invited him to Paris, where he began designing textiles and accompanying her to the famous costume balls of the era. Together, they set out to create a new look to complement her more casual approach to fashion. They created wide enamel

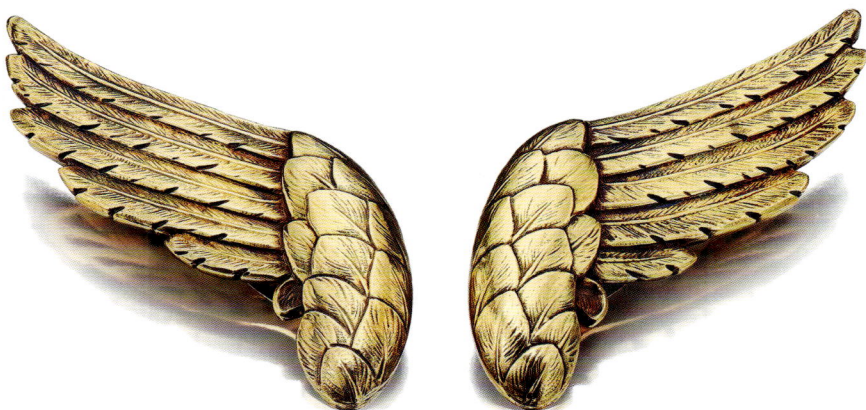

cuffs with Maltese crosses set with a rebellious mix of precious emeralds, rubies, sapphires and semi-precious amethyst, peridot and tourmaline. Chanel wore one on each wrist and, along with her ropes of pearls and chains, they became her signature; they also became a signature of the House.

Verdura came to America in 1934 and began working for Paul Flato. In 1939, his friends Cole Porter and Vincent Astor financed his debut on Fifth Avenue. Verdura's Italian background translated into designs that were inspired by classical patterns, but brightened with intense colours and a sophisticated

which she wore in publicity stills for her last film, *Two-Faced Woman* – are staples that influence jewellery design still to this day. Verdura also designed the large engagement ring worn by **Katharine Hepburn** in *The Philadelphia Story* (1940). In 1985, seven years after Fulco di Verdura's death, Ward Landrigan purchased the company. In 2014, Landrigan and his son Nico celebrated the House of Verdura's 75th anniversary on Fifth Avenue with an exhibition entitled 'The Power of Style: Verdura at 75'.

wit. During this time, Verdura designed pieces for some legendary actresses, which were also worn on film. In 1939, Brian Aherne purchased a pink topaz and diamond wing brooch for his wife, **Joan Fontaine**, which she wore in Hitchcock's 1941 film *Suspicion*. Verdura also created gifts for Linda Porter to give Cole Porter on the opening night of each of his Broadway shows.

While leading man **Tyrone Power** caught the eye of female movie-goers with his dashing good looks, he also became one of the stars that men wanted to emulate. For Christmas 1941 he gave his then wife, the French actress Annabella, an artfully flirtatious Verdura-designed 'Sash Heart' brooch with ruby cabochons and a gold bow. It was a romantic gesture and a gem of an idea.

Verdura's iconic curb-link bracelet and watch – designed for **Greta Garbo**,

It featured jewels from the private collections of **Sofia Coppola**, **Sarah Jessica Parker**, **Brooke Shields**, **Whoopi Goldberg** and **Barbara Taylor Bradford**.

In 2024, FX's limited series ***Feud: Capote Vs. The Swans*** streamed on Hulu on Thursday evenings. The jewels that reflect the time period and the styles worn by the socialites in the film were borrowed from Verdura. In the second episode, 'Babe' Paley (Naomi Watts) shows her jewellery to 'Slim' Keith (Diane Lane) and tells her which pieces were gifts for her husband Bill Paley's (Treat Williams) infidelities; to which 'Slim' replies: "The affairs end. But the jewellery remains!" When Duke Fulco di Verdura opened his salon on Fifth Avenue in 1939, he developed personal and professional relationships with several of the Swans discussed in the book

Capote's Women by Laurence Leamer, on which the series was based. 'Babe' Paley and Nancy 'Slim' Keith, in particular, were amongst Verdura's best clients and dearest friends. With this in mind, the Verdura brand issued a statement that they were "thrilled to loan many pieces from its collection to the costume department throughout the course of filming". When asked how producer and costume designer Lou Eyrich had worked with the House of Verdura to choose the pieces, she explained: "We often took the fitting photos to Verdura and picked accordingly, taking advice from the Verdura archivist Caroline Perkowski and team, who had an in-depth knowledge of the jewellery collection and style sensibilities of the Swans."

Eyrich also explained: "The jewellery in the series was in the style of actual pieces (using only a few of the archival pieces and then those remade with the same moulds as the originals) the Swans owned, and we tried to be period specific to the decades we were depicting." In the same scene as the Rubellite X bracelet, Babe shows Slim a ring "made to Bill [Paley's] specifications" – it is the vintage Verdura Raja ring with Ceylon sapphire and turquoise.

David Webb was another designer whose jewels spanned several decades

of the 20th century. Growing up in North Carolina, he was apprenticed to his uncle's silversmith shop where he learned metalsmithing techniques. Webb arrived in New York at the young age of 17 and got a job repairing jewellery in Greenwich Village. In 1948, after learning as much as he could as a bench jeweller, he founded the company that bears his name and opened a shop on Manhattan's Madison Avenue. He went on to help define the look of two decades in American cultural history (see Chapters 7–9).

Webb was 37 years old when Jackie Kennedy asked him to create the White House Gifts of State. The idea came about during a tour she made of the Smithsonian's Gem Hall. She asked David Webb to submit seven designs using minerals native to the United States. All seven designs were accepted, and many more followed. Webb also designed jewellery for the melodramas of the early sixties: **Susan Hayward** in *Backstreet*, **Lana Turner** in *Portrait in Black* (and later in *Madame X*), and **Doris Day** in *Midnight Lace*. His designs captured the essence of the characters. **Diana Vreeland**, **The Duchess of Windsor**, **Jackie Kennedy** and a host of socialites also wore his jewellery. The Duchess of Windsor called him "Fabergé reborn" and Jackie Kennedy referred to him as "a modern

day Cellini". In 2010, Mark Emanuel and Robert Sadian purchased the company in order to continue the David Webb legacy and bring the beauty and power of the designs to a modern-day customer. The business was then purchased in 2025 by Middle West Partners, who are committed to leading the House forward.

The legendary 'King of Diamonds' **Harry Winston** was also a major player providing inspiration and jewels for films during the 1950s and '60s. In *Gentlemen Prefer Blondes* (1953), **Marilyn Monroe**, as 'Lorelei Lee', let the world know that if it were diamonds a girl wanted, then there was a man she needed to know, when she belts out "talk to me Harry Winston, tell me all about it!" Winston bought and sold some of the world's rarest diamonds and his jewels played a supporting role to actresses such as **Ingrid Bergman**, who wore a Harry Winston necklace in the

1946 film *Notorious*. Winston's diamonds also appeared on **Anne Bancroft**'s 'Mrs. Robinson' in the 1967 cult favourite *The Graduate*. She wears a diamond bracelet, cluster earrings and a sizeable ring, which stays on throughout her scene with the young Dustin Hoffman. The ring was reportedly set with one of the 18 stones cut from the Lesotho rough diamond. Another of the stones, a 40.42-carat marquise, was given to **Jackie Kennedy** by Aristotle Onassis as an engagement ring.

Cartier was as much a part of the Hollywood dream factory as they were jewellers that helped to define the Art Deco period and cater to royalty and socialites of the 20th century. On the silver screen, as in real life, Cartier jewellery could be used to develop and define a character's personality.

A Cartier diamond bracelet features against the far darker backdrop of Hitchcock's World War II psychological drama *Lifeboat* (1944), based on a John Steinbeck story. In the first scene, 'Constance Porter', played by **Tallulah Bankhead**, appears in a lifeboat, amid a group of other survivors from a torpedoed ship, wearing a Cartier diamond bracelet. A famous reporter, she also has a camera, a fur coat, a gold cigarette case, a typewriter, a pocket flask of whiskey, and a handbag surrounding her. Her possessions gradually turn into necessities for survival, rather than the luxury items they once were. Eventually, the one possession she has left that she can offer the castaways – who are at this point starving – is the diamond bracelet. A gift from her first husband, it had functioned as a good luck charm for 15 years. The survivors want to catch fish, but realise they do not have anything to use as bait. 'Connie' removes the bracelet from her wrist and says: "Sure we have bait – by Cartier!" When one of the passengers asks: "Are you kidding?" she remarks: "Kidding my foot, I'm starving..." More conversation ensues and Connie adds, "I can recommend the bait. I ought to know... I bit on it myself." She then looks on, laughing, as the bracelet is washed away just at the point they think they have caught a fish.

In the 1956 MGM musical *High Society* – based on the play and earlier movie *The Philadelphia Story* – a piece of jewellery was written into the script. "Say, that's quite some rock you got there, Sam," says 'C.K. Dexter Haven' (played by Bing Crosby) to his ex-wife and socialite 'Tracy Samantha Lord' (Grace Kelly). He then turns to 'Tracy's' fiancé, and asks: "You mine that yourself, George?" 'Dexter' is referring to the 10.47-carat emerald-cut Cartier engagement ring adorning 'Tracy's' left hand. This was **Grace Kelly**'s own

engagement ring from Prince Rainier III, which she asked director Charles Walters if she could wear during the shooting of the film. The ring turned out to be a perfect fit for the part of a newly engaged socialite and appears often in the film, alongside Kelly and Crosby and co-stars Frank Sinatra and Celeste Holm.

Cartier received top billing in the opening credits of *How to Steal a Million*. A 1966 heist comedy, which lists Peter O'Toole and **Audrey Hepburn** in the lead roles, also announces 'Ms. Hepburn's jewelry by Cartier, Paris'. In various scenes in which the main protagonists meet to discuss how to perform the robbery, Hepburn wears Cartier diamonds and a Tank watch. In one scene, she appears in a lace mask and an epic pair of cluster diamond clip earrings that are as on point today as they were in the mid '60s. If only a line in the movie would have mentioned Cartier, all would have been complete. But the exchange between O'Toole ('Simon') and Hepburn ('Nicole') about her wardrobe (always by Givenchy, except for a few of her earliest films) was a great moment in throwaway lines that mostly only insiders and serious Hepburn fans will catch. As 'Nicole' changes into a cleaning-woman's costume for the heist, 'Simon' says: "Yes, that's fine. That does it."

'Nicole' replies: "Does what?"

'Simon' retorts: "Well, for one thing, it gives Givenchy a night off."

a real buzz at the time, with customers walking into Cartier boutiques requesting the 'Daisy Ring'.

I have seen **Gloria Swanson** as 'Norma Desmond' at least a half dozen times in the 1950 film *Sunset Boulevard* and have coveted her (own) 1930s Cartier rock crystal and diamond cuffs that she wears in the film and in many publicity shots for the movie. We see the bracelets on Swanson again after she is nominated for the Best Actress Academy Award for this film and is pictured waiting for the announcement of the results at a party in 1951. With her are Judy Holliday and José Ferrer, who are both also up for awards. Fortunately for them, they hear that they have won; unfortunately for Swanson, she has not.

Two more recent films that went from real life to the reel of film featured jewels by Cartier: *Grace of Monaco*, with **Nicole Kidman** playing the lead, and the Madonna-directed *W.E.*, starring **Andrea Riseborough** as Wallis Simpson. Cartier recreated all of the original jewels in precious metals and faux stones for both films in their London factories and then, when the film and publicity tours were over, destroyed them so they could never be copied or imitated.

In the 1974 version of *The Great Gatsby* film, starring **Mia Farrow** and Robert Redford, Cartier's designer Alfred Durante created many of the Art Deco pieces for Mia Farrow's wardrobe, including long ropes of pearls, sautoir necklaces, a diamond rivière, and long drop earrings. There were also Cartier brooches and clips, and sautoirs worn by Lois Chiles as 'Jordan Baker', as well as jewels designed for the film's extras. Perhaps the most important jewel in this film version is 'Daisy's' engagement ring: a marquise-shaped diamond set in platinum with a small diamond melée on each side of the shank. The ring created

There are some images that are inextricably tied to our collective consciousness – **Audrey Hepburn** standing in a black gown, long black gloves, faux diamond jewels and a tiara created a new era for the famed House of **Tiffany and Co.** Peering into the jewellery store's windows on Fifth Avenue, while eating a croissant and sipping coffee in the opening scene of *Breakfast at Tiffany's*, she created an aura around diamonds, pearls and the jewellery House and secured its place in movie history, as a tourist attraction and in the minds of all women who saw the film. Hepburn was also one of only four people ever to wear the 128-carat Tiffany Diamond, one of the largest and finest fancy yellow diamonds in the world. She wore it in 1961 for *Breakfast at Tiffany's* publicity shots, set into the Jean Schlumberger for Tiffany & Co. Ribbon Rosette necklace. (A politician's wife had previously worn the diamond to an official dinner in 1957.) Schlumberger also created a 'wardrobe of jewels' for the famed Tiffany Yellow Diamond. Another of his most famous settings for the diamond was the Bird on a Rock brooch. The gem was first discovered in the Kimberley diamond mine in South Africa in 1877.

The following year, the 287.42-carat stone was purchased by founder Charles Lewis Tiffany for $18,000. Dr George Frederick Kunz, Tiffany's chief gemmologist in Paris, supervised the cutting of the rough diamond into a cushion-shape brilliant weighing 128.54 carats with 82 facets – 24 more facets than the traditional brilliant cut – to enhance its beauty and vivid colour. The legendary diamond has been put up for sale just once in its history, but for some reason did not sell. In 2012, a necklace of 100 carats of white diamonds was created to celebrate the 175th anniversary of Tiffany & Co., and to honour the legacy of the jeweller's most famous gem. Lady Gaga wore this to the 91st Academy Awards ceremony to accept her Oscar for Best Original Song in 2019. And Beyoncé wore the diamond in a necklace in a Tiffany advertising campaign in 2021. More recently, in 2023, it was reset amid five flying diamond birds as a transformable brooch/pendant, in homage to Schlumberger's Bird on a Rock, and to celebrate the reopening of The Landmark on Fifth Avenue.

Jean Schlumberger was originally hired by legendary designer Elsa Schiaparelli to design buttons in the 1930s. During the time he worked for Schiaparelli, he went on to design costume jewellery.

In 1946, Jean Schlumberger opened a jewellery salon in Paris with his business partner Nicolas Bongard. Schlumberger was most inspired by sea life, mythological creatures, flowers and various forms of nature, always rendered with a bit of the fantastical or humour and wit. In 1956, he was invited to work with Tiffany & Co. by its then president, Walter Hoving. Schlumberger had his own workshop within the company and was eventually given the role of Vice President. He is one of only four designers Tiffany & Co. has ever allowed to sign their work.

Schlumberger created an intricately detailed diamond, sapphire and emerald brooch in the shape of a stylised dolphin, which Richard Burton gifted to Elizabeth Taylor in 1964 on the opening night of his film *The Night of the Iguana*. Taylor memorably wore it in her hair to a Lido première in Paris later that year.

Schlumberger's innovative enamel bracelets, in vivid red, blue and green spiked with gold, became so synonymous with **Jacqueline Kennedy** that the press dubbed them the 'Jackie bracelets'. **Lauren Bacall** was also a collector of Schlumberger. During the 1960s, she travelled regularly to Paris, and on those trips met and became friends with Jean Schlumberger, who kept a small boutique near the Grand Palais. Some of the famed actress's jewels, including many of the pieces she chose from Schlumberger, were sold as part of 'The Lauren Bacall Collection' at Bonhams New York in the spring of 2015. The Schlumberger 18K gold amethyst ring sold for $52,500, far in excess of the $8–12,000 estimate. One of the 18K yellow gold rope-work bracelets sold for $50,000.

When in Rome, everyone from international film stars to socialites stopped at **Bulgari** on the famed street Via Condotti close to the Spanish Steps. The global renowned luxury brand was founded by Sotirio Bulgari, who had begun his career selling jewellery at his family's shop in his native Greece. He moved to Italy and, in 1884, opened Bulgari in Rome as a single jewellery shop on Via Sistina. In 1905, he opened his flagship store on the Via Condotti, which was frequented by local clients, aristocrats and wealthy tourists. Originally a traditional Italian silversmith retailer, after the war Sotirio's sons Costantino and Giorgio began to

◀ Emerald and diamond convertible brooch-pendant set in platinum, 1958. Formerly in the collection of Elizabeth Taylor. © Bulgari Heritage Collection. Photo: Barrella – Studio Orizzonte Gallery

∨ Elizabeth Taylor dressed for the Lido premiere, wearing a Balenciaga sari and Jean Schlumberger for Tiffany's 'The Night of the Iguana' brooch in her hair, Paris, 1964. © TESSEYRE Jean / Paris Match Archive via Getty Images

take Bulgari in a more glamorous and contemporary direction. The jewellery was inspired by Greco-Roman Classicism and the Italian Renaissance, and Bulgari acquired important gemstones and created exclusive luxury pieces.

During the mid-20th century, many Hollywood movies were filmed in Italy, where production costs were lower. The stars on location began to shop at Bulgari, giving the company wider international recognition. **Tyrone Power and Linda Christian**, who married in Rome in 1949, purchased their wedding bands from Bulgari. While on location in Italy in 1962, **Elizabeth Taylor and Richard Burton** visited the Bulgari Via Condotti store, Burton buying Taylor gifts to celebrate their love affair. Later, in her book *My Love Affair with Jewelry*, she recalled: "Undeniably, one of the biggest advantages to working on *Cleopatra* in Rome was Bulgari's nice little shop". It was at this time that Taylor and Burton – both still married to other people – started their love affair. Burton was quick to pick up on the way to Taylor's heart, and quipped: "The only Italian Elizabeth knows is Bulgari." The Via Condotti store has been refurbished by architect Peter

Marino, but the room where Burton and Taylor used to choose jewels is still dubbed the 'salotto Taylor'. Taylor recalls in her memoir that Burton wanted to buy her a gift and so they headed over to Bulgari. They were shown two emerald necklaces, one with a detachable brooch with diamonds around it. Taylor chose the brooch. It was a step-cut Colombian emerald of 23.44 carats, created by Bulgari in 1958. Burton purchased it for her as a gift and the actress wore it on their wedding day in March 1964.

Soon after, she received the emerald necklace to which the brooch could be attached, which was mounted with 16 step-cut octagonal Colombian emeralds of an estimated total of 60.50 carats, each surrounded by brilliant-cut and pear-shaped diamonds. She also acquired a remarkable pair of diamond and emerald pear-shaped pendant earrings and a fantastic emerald and marquise-shaped diamond 'zigzag' bracelet, which Taylor said she liked to wear with the brooch.

She was then given an emerald ring set in platinum with a step-cut octagonal emerald of 7.40 carats surrounded with

pear-shaped diamonds to complete this parure. She would continue to wear pieces from her emerald collection for the rest of her life and particularly at some of the most important milestones. She also owned *en tremblant* pieces, including an emerald, platinum and diamond flower-head brooch, which had been given to her by former husband, Eddie Fisher. The flower spray, mounted on spring settings and shimmering

and flickering with every movement, was worn by Taylor in her hair, along with the earrings and the emerald step-cut brooch in the film *The V.I.P.S* with Richard Burton; she had previously worn the *en tremblant* piece on the occasion of receiving an award in 1960 for her role in *Suddenly, Last Summer*.

In 2011, Bulgari re-acquired eight pieces in total from the Christie's auction 'The Collection of Elizabeth Taylor'.

Mostly gifts from Richard Burton, these are now among the highlights in the Bulgari Heritage Collection, which also includes pieces that once belonged to Gina Lollobrigida.

In the 1950s, at the beginning of her acting career, **Gina Lollobrigida** was hailed as the most beautiful woman in the world. 'La Lollo's' smouldering glamour was matched by that of another Italian – the jewellery of Bulgari. One of her favourite pieces was a scroll-motif diamond and platinum necklace-and-bracelet combination created by the jeweller in 1954. It can also be worn as a tiara, as Lollobrigida did when she received her 1961 Golden Globe for World Film Favourite and, in 1964, in the movie *Woman of Straw*. Lollobrigida purchased many of her own jewels from Bulgari.

In 2013, as part of the auction house's 'Magnificent Jewels and Noble Jewels' sale, Sotheby's Geneva sold 23 of Gina Lollobrigida's Bulgari jewels, including a pair of natural pearl and diamond earrings that sold to an anonymous bidder for an unexpected £1.5 million. All of these jewels had been purchased and worn at the height of the actress's career and bought at various milestones in her life.

Sophia Loren was another legendary customer of the shop, as was **Anna Magnani**, another Italian actress who amassed a major collection of Bulgari jewels, which she purchased herself. From humble beginnings, Magnani worked her way through Rome's Academy of Dramatic Art by singing at nightclubs and in music halls. By 1955, she was awarded the Best Actress Oscar for her fearless and unforgettable performance as the grieving Sicilian widow in *The Rose Tattoo*. Tennessee Williams was said to have been so taken by her acting abilities that he wrote the play specifically for her. A strong, independent woman, Magnani had an intensity about her – like the characters she played. She made personal style statements with her jewellery, in particular the multiple Bulgari platinum curb-link bracelets.

The jewels and the iconic brands made famous by these legendary celebrities had a great influence on jewellery fashion and design at the time. For the collector who wants to relive the glamour of the Golden Age of Hollywood, the stars' jewellery, through the auctions of their personal collections, as well as similar vintage pieces, can be found on the market through dealers, high-end antique and vintage shops and trade fairs.

Bulgari convertible necklace-brooch-bracelets-tiara in platinum with diamonds, 1954. Formerly in the collection of Gina Lollobrigida. Private collection. Photography Barrella - Studio Orizzonte Gallery.

Cocktail Hour
The 1950s

The 1950s was a decade of optimism and prosperity both in the USA and Europe. The war years had ended and a new way of life started to emerge. In the States, suburban housing developments were sprouting up. There was a different outlook on women's roles – they no longer needed to work in factories, and marriage was on the rise among younger couples. Women were encouraged to be homemakers and raise families while their husbands went off to work so they could have what was considered the 'American Dream' – a more than comfortable lifestyle with the ability to purchase the latest and greatest cars

and appliances for the home. It was the cocktail party era, during which neighbours dressed up on weekends and got together at each other's homes. Or

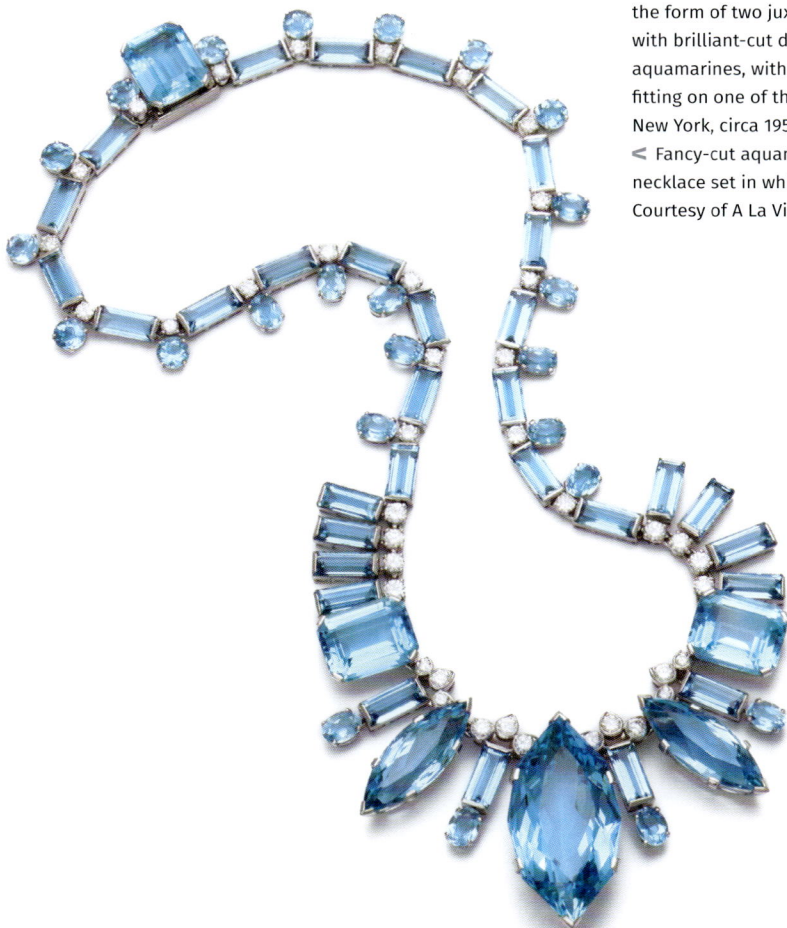

couples went out into the city to supper clubs, dancing, the theatre and nights on the town. In jewellery, although there was a comeback of the big three – sapphires, emeralds and rubies – semi-precious gems continued to be popular from the end of the 1940s and throughout the 1950s.

In the USA, it was also the Golden Age of TV – with shows like *Father Knows Best* and *Leave It To Beaver*, mirrors for the 1950s idealised lifestyle, depicting the different roles in the family that were usual for this era. In Europe, there was also a new found affluence, which was reflected in fashion such as Dior's New

< Burmese-ruby and diamond brooch, by Raymond Yard, circa 1950s. Courtesy of Fred Leighton
V Pair of ruby and diamond earrings set in platinum, Cartier, circa 1950. Courtesy of A La Vieille Russie
VV Ribbon bracelet, 1959. Platinum, yellow gold, Mystery Set rubies, diamonds. Van Cleef & Arpels Collection.
© Van Cleef & Arpels SA.

Look from 1947, which spilled over into the new decade and influenced trends in clothes and jewellery on both sides of the Atlantic.

Bill Rau, third generation owner of the shop M.S. Rau in New Orleans, explains: "After the years of WWII austerity, there was a real shift in the mood in the early 1950s. People were building new lives, and that feeling was reflected in the jewellery. It wasn't about practicality anymore; the jewellery of the era was about joy, exuberance, and expressing one's personality. It's important to remember the incredible craftsmanship behind these pieces too. The established European Maisons like Cartier and Van Cleef & Arpels were still at the top of their game, creating works of art. But there was also a rise in American jewellery designers who were pushing the boundaries of design and innovation. It was a truly exciting time in the jewellery world."

Hollywood also played a major role in influencing jewellery trends: stars such as Elizabeth Taylor, Grace Kelly, Audrey Hepburn, Marilyn Monroe and Sophia Loren were gracing the silver screen, wearing the jewels of iconic Maisons (see Chapter 4). The fresh designs of the well-established Houses, both in the USA and in Paris, as well as Bulgari in Rome,

> Gold-wire-twist, curb-link bracelet, by Georges L'Enfant for Tiffany & Co., 1950s. The bracelet featured on the cover of *Vogue New York* in October 1956. Courtesy of the Macklowe Gallery

V Turquoise and diamond bombé-cluster ring featuring turquoise cabochons, accented round- and single-cut diamonds mounted in 18K yellow gold and platinum, French, circa 1950s. Courtesy of Fred Leighton

>V Pair of diamond flower and leaf clip earrings, Cartier. Courtesy of A La Vieille Russie

a variety of different gemstones, cuts and configurations that were filled with character. These statement pieces were a way for women to show off their individuality and sophistication, especially during their glamorous weekend evenings out.

continued to be coveted by socialites and celebrities during this period of taste, style and different looks for day and night.

When the 1950s rolled around, there was a return to white gold and platinum, which had been restricted for much of the '40s due to the war effort. The styles of the decade were defined by statement pieces: chunky yellow gold, ribbons and bows made of precious metals, and diamonds set once again in white metal.

The cocktail ring was one of the main jewels of the period, which first appeared on women's fingers in the later Retro period. Different stones and three-dimensional motifs created a look that was exciting and featured

< Pair of swirl clip earrings, 18K yellow gold and platinum with pavé-set diamonds, by Cartier, London, circa 1950. Courtesy of A La Vieille Russie
V Diamond and platinum bracelet. The round- and baguette-cut diamonds create a graceful and elegant waving-fan pattern. This bracelet exemplifies the classic glamour of the 1950s. Courtesy of MS Rau

There was a clear division between night and day jewels, which had not been seen throughout the war years. Yellow gold was still popular for daytime, while white metals set with diamonds or precious stones took over the evening hours.

In the late 1940s, De Beers had run a series of ads with the slogan 'A Diamond is Forever', aimed at boosting engagement ring sales. The campaign was such a success that by the '50s dazzling diamonds were enjoying renewed popularity in all categories, with various shapes and cuts, such as marquises, baguettes, princess and pear cuts mixed in single pieces, reminiscent of Art Deco jewels.

The Van Cleef & Arpels 'Zip' Necklace

The fabric and textile trims we first saw in the 1940s also carried over into the '50s with ribbons, bows, knots, tassels and pleated, draped or seemingly ruched details. The most masterful design based on trims is the 'Zip' necklace by Van Cleef & Arpels.

It first originated in the late 1930s, when Renée Puissant, the Maison's Artistic Director and daughter of Alfred Van Cleef and Estelle Arpels, decided to create a jewel inspired by the zip fastener. They eventually produced the perfect necklace in 1950. An ingenious design, it actually opens and closes like a real zip and can be worn in two different ways: as a necklace or a bracelet, which is in keeping with the transformable jewellery of the day.

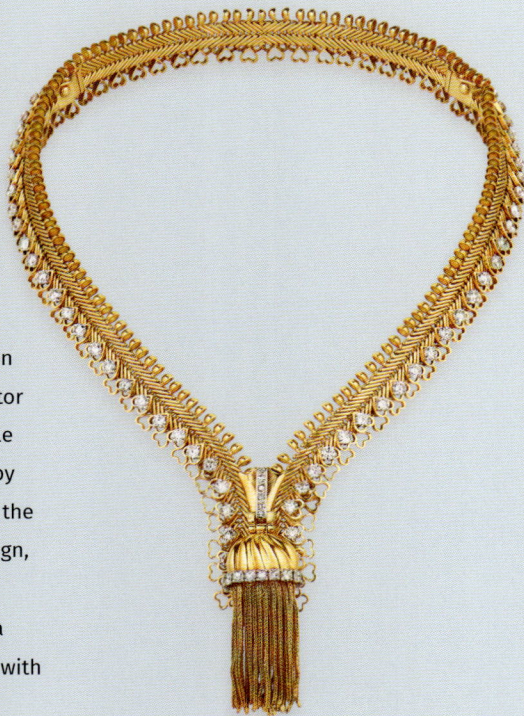

Λ Van Cleef & Arpels ingenious 'Zip' necklace, shown 'open' as a necklace, yellow gold, set with brilliant-cut diamonds, 1951. Van Cleef & Arpels Collection. © Van Cleef & Arpels SA.

V With the back section removed, the 'Zip' can be worn as a bracelet, 1951. Van Cleef & Arpels Collection. © Van Cleef & Arpels SA.

V Peridot and sapphire thistle earrings, each set with a brilliant-cut diamond, by Jean Schlumberger for Tiffany & Co., circa 1950. Courtesy of A La Vieille Russie
VV Flower brooch with pink topaz, aquamarine, diamond, emerald and platinum, by Verdura, circa 1957. © Verdura

The more structured styles of the '40s gave way to naturalistic forms in all types of animals, sea life, birds as well as botanicals and plant life. There was also a dash of whimsy seen in some of the motifs that captured the vivacity of the decade.

Some of the most popular pieces of jewellery were strings of pearls. These were an exception to the usual contrasting day/night styles, and could be worn anytime and for any occasion: from sweater sets or twin sets, to black cocktail dresses. Pearl earrings and brooches were also of the moment.

Inspiration came from different cultural aspects of the time. The overriding influences could be seen on the big screen on one of the most fashionable and iconic actresses of the times.

Grace Kelly became a poster girl for pearls in the 1950s. Women everywhere wanted to possess the style and elegance that Grace Kelly evoked as high society fashion model 'Lisa Fremont' in *Rear Window* (1954). In every scene she wears a different variation of pearls – chokers, graduated strands, earrings and a chunky charm bracelet. "I favour pearls on screen

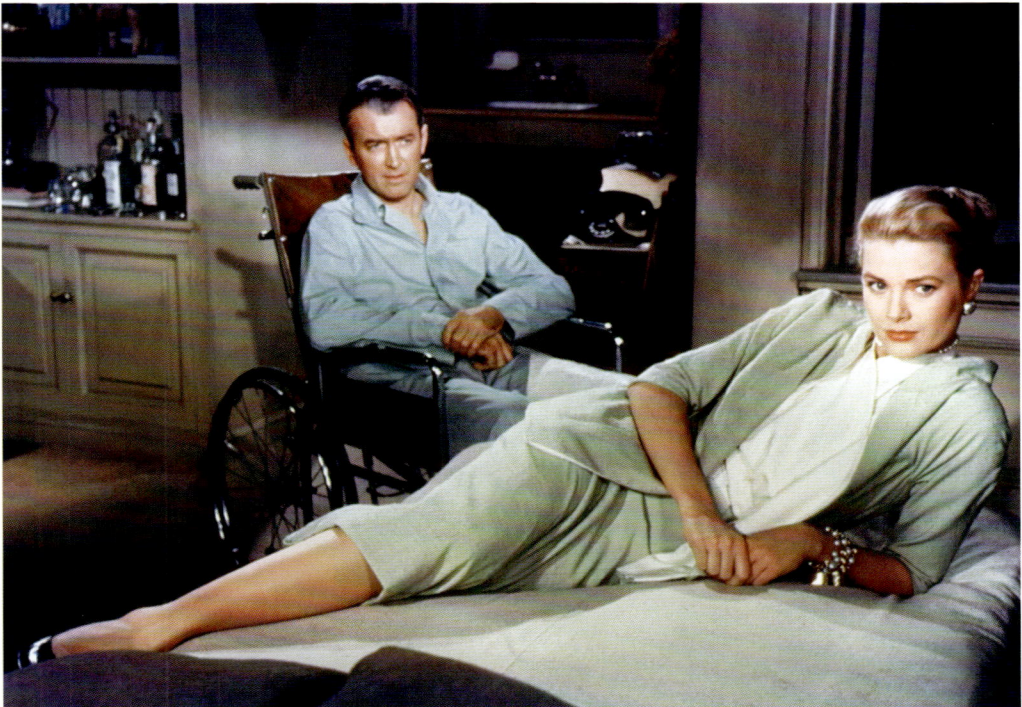

▼ Grace Kelly, wearing her pearl jewellery, with James Stewart in a scene from Hitchcock's *Rear Window*, 1954. © Paramount Pictures / Diltz / Bridgeman Images

and in my private life", she was quoted as saying. Lustrous, with a classicism that evoked true and natural elegance, pearls reflected Kelly's own luminescence. In her official engagement photo with Prince Rainier III, she wears a two-strand pearl choker. On her wedding day, she selected simple pearl and diamond earrings to complement her intricate lace gown.

As a wedding gift, Rainier commissioned a parure of pearls from Van Cleef & Arpels and, after their wedding at the Monaco Cathedral in April 1956, Van Cleef & Arpels became the jewellers to the Principality. Princess Grace's Van Cleef & Arpels pearl wedding suite consisted of a perfect pearl necklace, a floral-motif ring with a centre pearl, a triple-strand bracelet, and a pair of ear clips. All were accented by baguette- and brilliant-cut diamonds as part of the design, and on the clasp of the necklace and bracelet. In her always regal style, Princess Grace wore this suite of pearls for many years after her wedding.

What Grace Kelly did for pearls, Marilyn Monroe did for diamonds – bringing them into our collective consciousness as the smouldering blonde bombshell 'Lorelei Lee' in *Gentlemen Prefer Blondes* (1953). Although Monroe sings "diamonds are a girl's best friend", the jewels she's wearing in the film are faux. Slinking around in a tight pink gown and long gloves – and dripping in imitation diamonds – she is dazzling as she sings out the names of the diamond designers of the day: "Tiffany's!... Cartier! Black, Starr, Frost, Gorham! Talk to me Harry Winston..."

Elizabeth Taylor, another iconic actress of the day, owned an amazing and aspirational jewellery collection that was legendary (see Chapter 5). She wore her jewels, like many actresses of the day, on and off screen, elevating the styles of what women would emulate in their daily lives.

Suites and demi suites – mostly earrings and necklaces or necklaces and bracelets – returned during this time period, primarily to complement evening wear. They featured either diamonds in different cuts and configurations or small cuts with larger coloured gemstones. Many had the same patterns as the brooches, with tactile elements or ribbon, mesh and fringe and were statement-making pieces. Necklaces were choker or swag styles, worn higher on the neck, punctuated by different cabochons mixed in with faceted diamond cuts; turquoise was one of the predominant stones. Bracelets were flexible and soft, feeling like fluid fabric on the wrist, or were links. Clip earrings were designed in either bold and powerful motifs of nature or swirls and ribbons; gemstones set in yellow gold were popular for day wear, while earrings designed for the evening included pendant and swinging chandelier styles in either platinum or white gold set with diamonds.

< Pair of turquoise and diamond clip earrings by Cartier. Courtesy of A La Vieille Russie
V Cartier citrine, diamond and ruby bracelet, set in yellow gold, circa 1950. Courtesy of MS Rau

The 1950s was the decade of the statement cocktail ring, designed to be seen from across the room. My grandmother was a great fan of cocktail rings. I remember her telling me how she got them in the '50s, but they had become so much a part of her personal style that she continued to wear them throughout the different decades. As a young girl, I tried them on at her house, big colourful rings that would fall off my fingers the minute I put them on. Turquoise, coral, opal and aquamarine with diamond accents were her favourites and were some of the predominant styles of the day. When I see them on the market today, I am reminded of her choosing only one cocktail ring on her right hand; on her left hand was the discreet wedding band and engagement ring my grandfather could afford that she would wear with pride and love.

As is often the way with popular fashion items, cocktail rings went out of style, and sadly many were simply melted down or the stones removed and reset into more modern jewellery. Those that were transformed into more contemporary designs were done by dealers when the quality of the stone outweighed the design sensibility. But this has always been the case when family members pass down jewellery from one generation to the next. The newest generation, who wants to keep

> Black opal and diamond cluster ring. Courtesy of A La Vieille Russie
V Siberian amethyst and diamond cocktail ring, American, circa 1950. Courtesy of A La Vieille Russie

the sentimentality of the ring, will reset the stone in a style more in keeping with their personality. But there are still a number of original cocktail rings on the market, more often than not signed pieces from the renowned Houses. Every now and then you can find some special rings with the stones of the era in excellent condition. It is a matter of scouting around.

One of the more youthful jewellery rituals of the 1950s was associated with the act of going steady. In the USA, high school and college kids professed their commitment to dating each other exclusively. The jewellery that was given by the boy to the girl was either a school ring or a pin. Going steady was one of the themes in the musical movie *Bye Bye Birdie*, in which 'Hugo' (Bobby Rydell) gives 'Kim' (Ann-Margret) his pin. At the beginning of the film there was a song 'The Telephone Hour' and some of the lyric include: 'Have you heard about Hugo and Kim? Did they really get pinned?' And then the song goes on from there. High school rings can still be spotted on the vintage market, although they are a rare find.

During the 1950s, charms and charm bracelets became one of the most

versatile and saleable pieces of jewellery (see Chapter 6). There were charms to celebrate and remember all occasions – for whatever could be imagined. They became popularised during the war years and then took off in the '50s with a vengeance in both in the United States and in Europe.

Charmed, I'm Sure
1940s and 1950s Charms

> First Lady Mamie Eisenhower's charm bracelet that
commemorated the important milestones in her life.
©Christie's Images/Bridgeman Images
V 14K gold charm set with coloured stones and engraved
with '*Je t'aime*' (I love you). Courtesy of Amie Park
VV 14K gold gem-set charm, by Henry Dankner & Sons.
Courtesy of Keyamour

From the jewellery featured on celebrities and style arbiters to pieces our First Ladies donned in real life and publicity stills, the '50s heralded the return of celebratory and sentimental charms not seen since the Victorian era. After WWII, there was a new light-hearted feeling that spread throughout the country, influencing mothers, their daughters, sisters and female friends and peers. In effect, every woman desired a charmed life or charms dangling from bracelets commemorating significant moments and occasions.

Additionally, suburban life with its cocktail parties and activities that revolved around family led to charms that reflected an abundance of styles, representing everything from travel and vacation spots to hobbies, sports, birthdays, anniversaries and the birth of children.

First Lady Mamie Eisenhower was the embodiment of the optimism of the '50s. She was cheerful, lively and also fashionable. She wore mink stoles, fitted hats, fit-and-flare dresses and a charm bracelet commemorating her life as a First Lady and her marriage to Ike. The bracelet, which included charms marking D-Day, Ike's presidential win and even a miniature of his West Point class ring, sold for $20,000 at Christie's 'Magnificent Jewels' sale in December 2017.

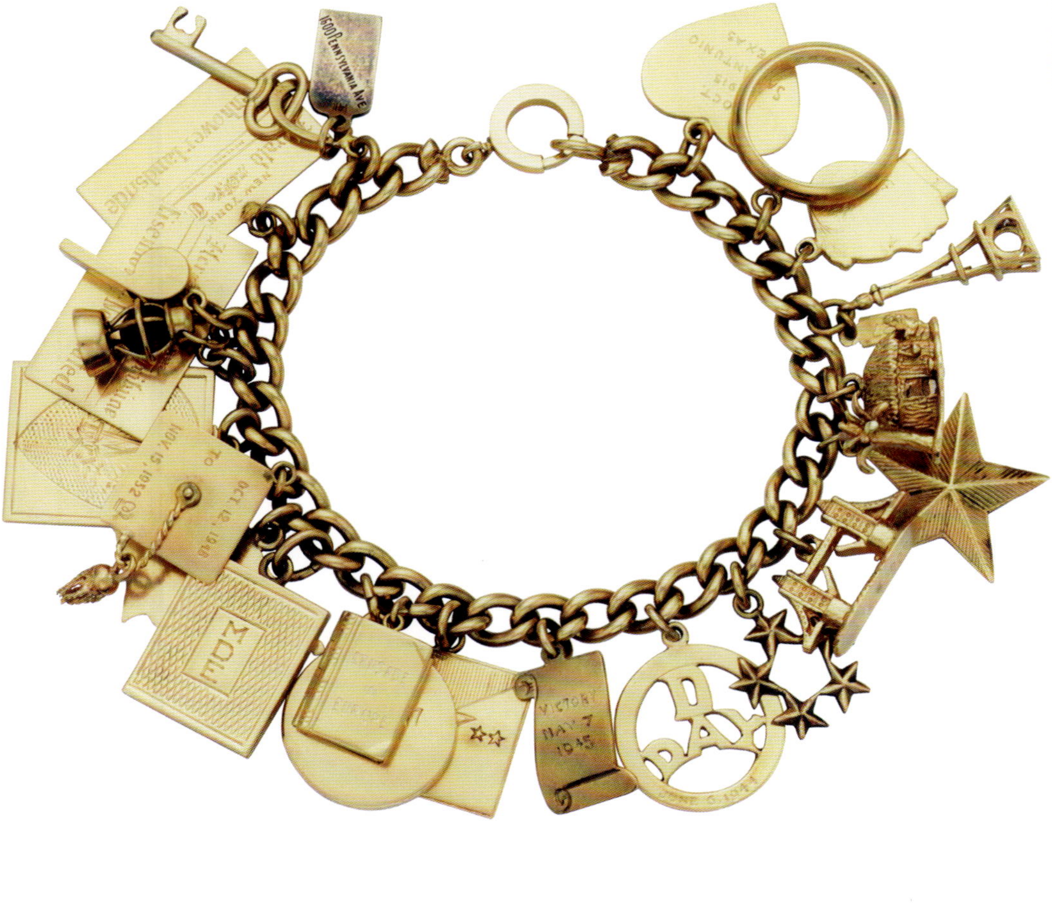
1600 PENNSYLVANIA AVE
VICTORY MAY 7 1945
D DAY

< 14K gold sewing machine charm with moving wheel and needle, mid-20th century. Courtesy of The Gold Hatpin
<V 14K gold rotary telephone charm with spinning dials that spell out "Hello" and "I Love U", mid-20th century. Courtesy of The Gold Hatpin
VV 14K gold Hope chest with enamelled man/husband inside, mid-20th century. Courtesy of The Gold Hatpin

Susan Cohen of Circa 1700, a designer and dealer who specialises in mid-20th century to early 1980s pieces explains: "When the war ended, the new decade saw a movement towards charms that recognised the growing middle class and symbolised ingenuity and innovation. There was more disposable income and modern technology was a way to make life easier for women who were homemakers. Charms representing so many aspects of a woman's life also made it easy for men to select gifts for every occasion imaginable." She continues: "Suddenly, little televisions dangled from women's wrists along with cameras, various types of automobiles, typewriters, and even refrigerators, freezers and other gadgets – all with moving knobs, wheels and even flaps that revealed little hidden secrets. We also saw the celebration of global travel with the creation of charms with airport codes, plane tickets, enamel maps of states and countries, and spinning globes dotted with gemstones where the wearer had ventured. Finding these vintage charms takes on new meaning today when it resonates with the collector's or wearer's individual moments and memories. It's a rich tapestry that celebrates the past while giving a nod to one's own personal achievements."

> 14K gold 'love' charm, circa 1950s. Courtesy of Lee Krombholtz
V Globe charm, 14K gold, 1950s. Courtesy of Wilson's Estate Jewelry
V> 14K gold Queen Mary cruise-ship charm, circa 1950s. Courtesy of The Gold Hatpin

Alice Kwartler is a retired Madison Avenue shop owner with 40 years' experience and expertise. As proprietor of Alice Kwartler Antiques, thousands of charms passed through her hands. She explains: "We came full circle from Queen Victoria's time to the 1950s when it was once again a time of wearing charms that represented a sentimental journey of a woman's life. However, the charms in the late '40s and throughout the '50s were much different. They were bolder, bigger, and many of them were designed with mechanical parts that rendered them meaningful and also unique and playful at the same time. Some of my personal favourites were tongue-in-cheek." She continues, "and some of our most famous actresses wore them, which made them all the more desirable."

Natalie Wood, Sophia Loren, Elizabeth Taylor and Lucille Ball were all famous owners of charm bracelets, who collected bespoke charms that had true emotional value and also provided a dose of high style in the '50s. Elizabeth Taylor wore her own charm bracelet in the film *Giant* in 1956. Taylor had worn charm bracelets as a girl and then well into womanhood.

A few of Taylor's charm bracelets were sold at the famous Christie's New York sale, 'The Collection of Elizabeth Taylor: The Legendary Jewels' in December 2011.

One deeply personal piece represented myriad mementos: gifts from directors she had worked with, such as Franco Zeffirelli; keepsakes of love from Richard Burton; rare charms, such as a Henry VIII gold half-sovereign of 1544–57 and a Napoleon Bonaparte medallion; heart-shaped lockets and charms and, perhaps the most personal, a locket inscribed with the names of her children.

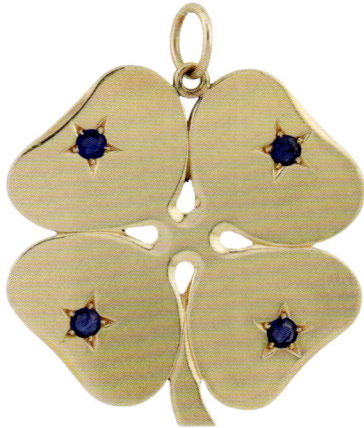

Dana Kiyomura of Keyamour agrees. "I see such intricate and wide range of charms and some of my all-time favourites are those that are mechanical or huge and three-dimensional. Those that are most desirable among my customers are always the styles with the most meaning."

Kwartler cites three-dimensional sailboats under the Moon and stars, and those which have mechanisms that allow them to open to reveal a secret inside. She adds: "But the jewellers of the time were also re-imagining charms that had to do with luck and protection in addition to romance and love which never went away."

For young girls and teenagers, the charm bracelet was the big craze of the 1950s. To own one began a rite of passage. And many of those girls added to the bracelets as they grew into adults. "The number of charms that were made during the decades between the '40s and '50s was amazing," says Elizabeth Doyle of Doyle & Doyle. "You could have a charm that represented every minor to the major occasion. You could find smaller styles for young girls that represented friendship, birthdays, graduations, hobbies, summer vacations, school supplies, sweet sixteen and much more. For women, there was every celebratory charm you could imagine."

Life was recorded and chronicled on a woman's wrist.

> 18K gold charm set with coral and turquoise hearts, by Cartier. Courtesy of Keyamour
∨ 14K gold 'I love you' puzzle with ruby bail, by Henry Dankner & Sons, circa 1950s. Courtesy of Amie Park

The designs of renowned Houses of the day that created charm bracelets provided a dose of high style and also a dash of wit and whimsy. Such Houses included David Webb, William Ruser, Paul Flato, Cartier, Van Cleef & Arpels and Tiffany & Co. But women could also find the charms at various price points. There was something for everyone and many can still be found on the market today.

Henry Dankner & Sons was one of the major players in the charm market and well known at the time for its large intricate charms; particularly those that were mechanical. Three of the

company's distributors included Cartier, Van Cleef & Arpels and Harry Winston. After fleeing Nazi Germany in 1944 after everything was seized from his Budapest workshop, Henry Dankner relocated to New York City, and in the 1950s restarted the company. He brought his two sons Robert and George in to learn the business and they kept it going until 2014. When the business closed, after six decades of design, the company donated all its archival sketches and moulds to the jewellery department at The Fashion Institute of Technology in order to preserve its legacy.

Amie Park, a dealer who has collected charms throughout her career, seeks out the most iconic charms from Houses such as Dankner, Cartier and Van Cleef & Arpels.

"When I started collecting 10 years ago, they were much easier to find. Recently, it took me two years to find one of the Dankner charms for which I had been searching. They have gone way up in price as they become more difficult to locate." She continues: "For the past 15 or so years, women have been collecting them to wear as charm necklaces, more so than bracelets, providing a new life for them. And, due to social media, Instagram and the internet, people have become more savvy about the rarer pieces."

Park remembers the sound of her grandmother's charm bracelet and holds those memories dear. I, too, remember the sound of my grandmother's and mother's bracelets and I keep a part of them always with me, wearing their charms mixed with those I have collected – a wearable memoir of precious moments, a record of who I am, my past, my present and what I hope for my future."

Susan Cohen, who in addition to being a jewellery designer and dealer is also a screenwriter and television producer, has found unique one-of-a-kind charms for TV and movie buffs. "These include styles with a little vintage clapboard and a little strip of film, various gold and enamel vintage network cameras and network logos: NBC, ABC and CBS."

She continues: "That lead me down an unexpected path of collecting vintage gold 'Oscar' charms, which were custom made for Academy Award winners. I've had the extremely good fortune to find several from the '50s, including one inscribed with "William Lyon – From Here To Eternity – 1953", and another for Best Song inscribed "High Hopes – 59" (by Frank Sinatra). Over the years, I've also

V 14K gold 'Oscar' charm. The 'Oscar' charm is believed to have originally been a party favour at the Oscar Governors Ball in the 1940s. Some years later a tradition began where Oscar winners were allowed to request a special 1"-tall miniature gold "Oscar" charm for each award that they won. Each charm was engraved on the bottom with the name of the recipient, the film, and the year of release. Courtesy of Circa 1700

sourced many of these for my clients in the entertainment business as lucky talismans."

The popularity of charm bracelets began to decline by the '60s, although there were other styles of charms being made that signified the decade, such as astrological charms. The personal charm bracelets of the '50s found their way to the dark recesses of jewellery boxes or were sold to savvy vintage dealers who kept them in their safes, or melted them down as scrap to buy other pieces that were more in favour at the time.

But the dealers who did hold on to them understood the idea of fine jewellery's cyclical nature, and that is why there are still signed and unsigned charms out there. Fast forward to modern times, and these little keepsakes of memories and moments, art and sentiment, luck and protection have become the gold standard of style once again. They might take patience and perseverance to score and require a higher price than you originally planned to pay, but many are still on the market today, and I think they are worth it.

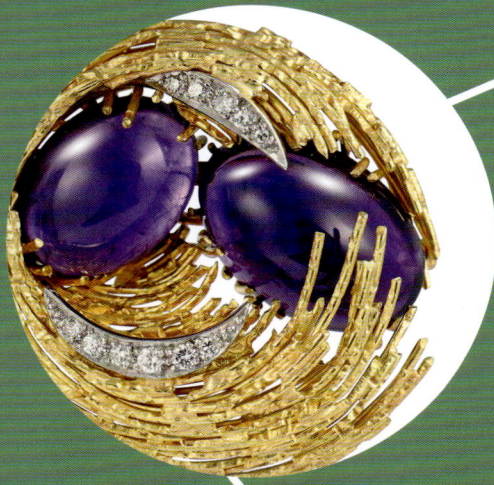

The Times They Are a-Changin'
The 1960s part 1

The 1960s was a monumental period: historically, politically, culturally, socially and artistically. It was also a time of international influences that produced radical changes and revolutionary ideas, setting the zeitgeist of the decade.

Politically in the USA, we saw the civil rights movement, the Kennedy and Martin Luther King Jr. assassinations, the Vietnam War, protests, and the sexual revolution that reverberated across the Atlantic.

Some of the profound inspirations in artistic endeavours sprang from London's Swinging Sixties and artist jewellers. The Paris fashion and jewellery industry looked towards what Diana Vreeland (editor-in-chief of *Vogue* at the time) coined the 'youthquake' – a movement initiated by young people's values, tastes and pop culture references. Other influences affecting the decade were Op Art and second-wave feminism. All of

these stimuli prompted individualism and led women to begin buying their own jewellery, fashion and accessories as a statement of their own identity.

In the USA, David Webb, Jean Schlumberger for Tiffany & Co., and Verdura were also affected by cultural and artistic changes and began designing for the new generation, as well as offering alternatives that would be accepted and desired by their loyal clientele of American socialites and celebrities. The same was true of Bulgari in Rome.

Towards the end of the decade, we saw the emergence of the anti-establishment 'hippies', who took over where the youthquakers left off. The Summer of Love, Woodstock, and the Moon landing – all translated into fashion and jewellery.

Born in the 1960s, I was too young to take in the events shaping the time period. But by the mid to latter part of the decade I began to understand certain parts of my parents' concerned discussions about the Vietnam War, and their horrified tears watching John F. Kennedy get shot on national TV. And their profound sadness again when Martin Luther King Jr. and Robert Kennedy were both assassinated.

I was still in elementary school, but I experienced many of the changes that took place throughout the world through my mom, dad, my aunts and uncles, on television, the music that was on the radio, and the albums that my dad brought home for me as gifts.

As events unfolded around the world, they each contributed to the rebellious, innovative and iconoclastic styles of the 1960s.

Adam Patrick from A La Vieille Russie notes: "Throughout the different periods, jewellery has taken its cue from fashion and complemented the different styles of the times." He continues: "When we examine the '60s decade, it is really

two distinct parts. The early years were adaptations of the styles introduced in the '50s. And then, starting in 1965, there is a radical shift for which the decade is more famously known. Hemlines pushed limits: first being knee length and then rising higher and higher with the mini skirt coming on the scene and more revealing and bolder fashions taking over the runways, magazines and high society. In the later part of the decade, around 1967, internationally, people wanted to express themselves. Therefore, you have

jewellery designers of the decade moving away from what is 'expected' and, instead, mixing unconventional combinations of different finishes and stones."

Patrick continues: "People are now collecting the work from this period; they see the value in the craftsmanship and the inventiveness."

Such were the cases of American jeweller Arthur King and, in France, Pierre Sterle, among many others who created pieces that were inspired by nature – from the sea to the sky – but with a subversive, sometimes asymmetrical, and oftentimes oversized and futuristic approach to fine jewellery.

The artist jeweller was not only accepted but caught the attention of the main Parisian established brands, including Chaumet, Van Cleef & Arpels, Cartier and Chopard, as well as Bulgari in Italy.

London Calling

In London, fashion designers were pushing boundaries to accommodate the new generation who were coming into their own, desiring pieces that were untraditional and less stuffy than they were used to seeing. The boom in the ready-to-wear market fuelled progressive boutiques such as Mary Quant (who is credited with the invention of the mini skirt), Biba, Ossie Clark, and other stores sprouting up on Carnaby Street and the King's Road. Much of the fashion was mass produced so that it would become more accessibly priced for the youth market that was driving the fresh looks, along with Op Art and the music scene. Bold graphic prints, vibrant colours, hot pants, babydoll and A-line dresses and wide-legged trouser suits were all the rage in fashion, in what would come to be known as the Swinging Sixties in 1966. David Bailey's photographs and models such as Jean Shrimpton, Twiggy, Penelope Tree and Edie Sedgwick, as well as actress Jane Birkin, all became the icons associated with '60s style splashed on the cover of magazines. Julie Christie, in the 1965 film *Darling*, encapsulated the look of the times, with Julie Harris receiving the Oscar for best costume design for the film.

Much of the jewellery during this time in London was made of lucite and plastics and were worn as fashion accessories. But, as collector and jewellery historian Kimberly Klosterman explains, there were also the avant-garde styles of "the 'artist jewellers' of the time".

Nonconformist and radical in their approach to creating pieces that were anything but traditional, they were similar to the revolutionary jewellers of

the Art Nouveau period, who rebelled against mass-produced industrial-age jewellery and worked with unorthodox materials for fine jewellery to create naturalistic and sometimes surreal pieces. "Their pieces created a movement in jewellery that represented the changing times," says Klosterman. "The group considered themselves artists first and jewellers second."

Bringing more attention to this group of artist designers was the 1961 International Exhibition of Modern Jewellery 1890–1961 curated by Graham Hughes, the art director of London's Goldsmiths' Hall. "He invited an international set of artists and jewellers to show their contemporary designs alongside historical pieces." Klosterman continues: "The time was ripe for these

< Monumental bombé-cluster ring set with seven moonstones and ten diamonds in a gold ball mount, English, circa 1960. Courtesy of A La Vieille Russie
> Brooch depicting a bird's nest of finely woven 18K gold, with diamond accents on either side, and two cabochon amethysts representing eggs within, by Andrew Grima, marked "HJC" (Grima's father's manufacturing company), English, circa 1965. Courtesy of Sandra Cronan
V Gold pendant/brooch set with cabochon sapphires and brilliant-cut diamonds, by Andrew Grima, circa 1968. Collection of Kimberly Klosterman, Photography by Tony Walsh, Courtesy of the Cincinnati Art Museum

artist jewellers to be launched into the spotlight as well as retail stores in the new social and cultural climate. English designers such as David Thomas, Andrew Grima, Gerda Flöckinger and John Donald were part of the exhibition and also showed the type of jewellery that would express individuality and personality of the wearer."

Many of these jewellers worked with heavily textured or rough-hewn gold and uncut, rough or unusual gemstones. Grima would go to the countryside to find naturalistic materials to cast into gold. His work received orders from the Royal family; Princess Margaret and Princess Anne both owned his pieces. One of Queen Elizabeth II's favourite brooches was her 'Ruby Venus' brooch by Grima, which was given to her by husband Prince Phillip.

Patrick from A La Vieille Russie adds: "You also have David Thomas creating pieces with raw crystals and citrines, something you would not have seen previously. The David Thomas ring is a great example. The mount is designed beautifully, the gems appear to be extensions of the mount. This was not seen in previous times."

Travel was popular during the '60s and the monied jet set – who wanted cutting-edge designs they could wear day or night, and be comfortable in while on a plane or visiting different cities – became fans of these jewellers. Since the pieces were not set with precious gems, they were easy to don without fear of theft, and also bigger and bold enough to pair with different outfits so the owners would not need to travel with too much.

The jewellers of the realm also designed pieces that were convertible (which has been an ongoing trend through different time periods prior to and during the 20th century). Necklaces split into bracelets, earrings were detachable, ring stones were interchangeable. Diamonds were used as accents to imbue the pieces with sparkle, although for the most part everything was tactile yellow gold with crystals, geodes and other materials.

We'll Always Have Paris

The fashion Houses, as well as the renowned jewellery brands in Paris, were also inspired by the youth culture, the graphic nature of Op Art, the Space Age, and what was going on in London on a cultural and aesthetic level.

Pierre Cardin, André Courrèges, Paco Rabanne and Yves St Laurent all produced their own versions of the mini skirt, short shift dresses, and wide-leg pantsuits. Courrèges's shift dresses with plastic paillettes and metallics became instantly recognisable and still are today, as are Paco Rabanne's Space Age and chain-mail dresses. The allure of appealing to a youthful audience resulted in many of the Parisian couturiers launching ready-to-wear collections.

On the jewellery front, established jewellery Houses were also ready to appeal to the youth culture, but without losing their regular clientele; so, they adopted styles of the times for both.

Highlights from Van Cleef & Arpels in the early to mid-'60s featured twist parures, which combined ornamental stones, pearls and yellow-gold beads. They were designed in coral, lapis lazuli, turquoise or chrysoprase, and gave a nod to the more casual looks of the times as well as the colour and movement that was so prevalent during this decade. These were shown in Van Cleef & Arpels's La Boutique on the Place Vendôme.

They were the first of the legendary jewellery Houses to open a separate boutique, in 1954, and, by the 1960s, the boutique line was a huge success, also housing a menagerie of animal brooches. These whimsical and fun interpretations were first shown in the '50s and grew to include more exotic, charming and sometimes mischievous animals such as lions, owls, monkeys and giraffes, which were crafted from yellow gold and accented with precious and semi-precious gemstones.

Unexpected cuts of faceted and cabochon combinations, as well as adventurous colour mixing, defined both the Maison and boutique jewellery of the time in every classification of jewellery. It also punctuated motifs that included flowers as well as Asian inspirations.

When In Rome

Bulgari had its own instantly recognisable style in the 1960s. The House broke away from its high-jewellery emerald, ruby and sapphire looks with diamond surrounds, and was inspired to create vivid colour schemes along the same lines as the Florentine designer Pucci's psychedelic and vivacious prints. They opened a new chapter of unyielding creativity with bold and fresh new combinations of semi-precious and precious cabochons and faceted stones in yellow gold – the mix of cut and colour gave the pieces a three-dimensional look, as youthful as it was chic.

Floral brooches in the Giardinetto style of earlier periods also came back during this time, but with cabochon and carved gemstones in the centre of the petals or the bottom of the flowerpot. *En tremblant* brooches were a speciality of the House and continued to flutter in emeralds and diamonds, similar to the brooch that Eddie Fisher gave Elizabeth Taylor when they were married.

Elizabeth Taylor's Watch

The Bulgari 'Serpenti' watch Elizabeth Taylor wore while on the set (but not in the film) of *Cleopatra* was the perfect example of the first models made in the early '60s. Specifically designed for her by the Maison, it was in yellow gold with emerald eyes, and diamonds in the head and tail of the serpent. Soon after, variations with and without the watch itself were created, and the company became more inventive with larger scales, single-colour and striking multi-colour enamel combinations, and diamond or gemstone eyes. Those that slithered and spiralled up the wrist were most eye-catchingly dramatic. The creation of the body of the bracelet was painstakingly elaborate, which was apparent in each one that was made.

∧> 'Serpenti' tubogas bracelet-watch in gold and platinum with emeralds and diamonds, circa 1961. Formerly in the collection of Elizabeth Taylor. Private Collection.

> Elizabeth Taylor on the set of *Cleopatra* wearing her Bulgari 'Serpenti' watch, Cinecetta Studio, Rome, 1962. © Associated Press/Alamy Stock Photo

Snakes became synonymous with Bulgari during this decade with the House's 'Serpenti' collection. The first snake-shaped bracelet watches were featured in the 1940s in Bulgari's tubogas technique. However, in the 1960s, the design of the 'Serpenti' collection evolved to become more realistic, with intricate scales and colours. Ingeniously, Bulgari concealed the watch (case and dial) in the snake's hinged head.

Iconic figure and editor-in-chief of American *Vogue* at the time, Diana Vreeland owned a serpent belt with pastel-and-white coloured enamel. She wore her jewels big and bold, and often wore the belt wrapped around her neck. In September of 1968, Vreeland sent one of the many memos she wrote during her tenure at *Vogue*, which read: "Don't forget the serpent… The serpent should be on every finger and on all wrists and everywhere. The serpent is the motif of Horus in jewellery. We cannot see enough of them."

As time went on, Bulgari explored a plethora of versions in which the case and dial – in myriad shapes – were placed in different positions other than the head, moving to the centre or end of the bracelet. It included watch movements from companies such as Audemars Piguet, Jaeger LeCoultre, Movado and Vacheron Constantin.

Bulgari's 'Monete' collection made its first appearance in the 1960s with antique coins mounted into modern jewellery forms, but became even more popular in the '70s (see Chapter 10).

< Gem- and diamond-set 'Marine Creature' demi-parure, by Schlumberger for Tiffany & Co., France, circa 1960. © Sotheby's

> Enamel, yellow sapphire, ruby and coral 'Parrot' clip-brooch, by Schlumberger for Tiffany & Co., France, circa 1960s. © Sotheby's

∨ Flower bracelet of a double coil of 18K gold wire, mounted with overlapping blossoms formed of marquise-cut citrines, pink and green tourmalines, and peridots, centred by round brilliant-cut diamonds, by Jean Schlumberger for Tiffany & Co., circa 1960s. Courtesy of the Macklowe Gallery

New York State of Mind

Although women from the middle classes through to socialites wore the fashions from the major designers in London and Paris, the USA had its own range of alternative designers, such as Betsey Johnson, Oleg Cassini, Giorgio di Sant' Angelo and Rudi Gernreich – who were all on target with the trends of the decade.

The jewellery of Verdura continued to evolve and attract socialites. And David Webb, who took off during the 1950s, flourished during this time period, along with Jean Schlumberger, who was designing for Tiffany and Co.

On a par with the Parisian jewellers, American designers were creating for women who wanted individuality as

Schlumberger's innovative enamel bracelets, in different colours spiked with gold, became so synonymous with Jacqueline Kennedy that the press dubbed them the 'Jackie bracelets' (see Chapter 5). For many style icons, they became *the* piece in which to be seen.

Levi Higgs, Head of Archives and Brand Heritage of David Webb since 2013, sees the height of Webb's career starting with the 1960s and evolving into the '70s. Says Higgs: "David Webb started being featured in many editorials during the 1960s and went on to win fashion's coveted Coty American Fashion Awards in 1964, which were also given to jewellers. Webb was only the second jeweller to win the award. This type of recognition really started to make the company roar. This was a time when he was allowing his vivid imagination to take over and experiment with different styles that were bold in scale, oftentimes witty and mixing different ancient cultures." Higgs notes that David Webb explained in 1967, a time of political upheaval in the USA: "There is nothing delicate about life today. It is elegant and harsh at the same time. Today's jewellery, like today's fashions, must eliminate the frivolities of life."

opposed to status and who had the disposable income to commission or purchase their designs. The jewels of Verdura, Webb and Schlumberger also employed the use of non-traditional materials, playful or eccentric colour combinations, and whimsical takes on animals, sea life and cross-cultural designs.

Schlumberger, who had been designing for Tiffany & Co. since 1956, was inspired by mythological creatures and all forms of nature. During the '60s, he created dolphins, sea urchins and starfish, set with unusual combinations of gemstones and brightly coloured enamel, all with a bit of the fantastical and his brand of humour and wit.

And so he drew upon his playful nature to design pieces that would be neither political nor frivolous but did on occasion have what Higgs calls "a cheekiness to them". His animal bracelets were rendered in different variations of coloured stones, enamel and yellow gold that were stunning in their effect of mixed materials and colour combinations.

Webb won the hearts of renowned women, including Jackie Kennedy, The Duchess of Windsor, Diana Vreeland, Elizabeth Taylor, Nan Kempner, Gloria Vanderbilt and a veritable roster of who's who of social and style fame. His society clientele in Palm Beach led him to opening a Worth Avenue salon in the early 1960s.

In 2013, three years after Mark Emanuel, Sima Ghadamian and Robert Sadian acquired the David Webb company, David Webb's New York store, once situated on East 57th Street, moved to 942 Madison Avenue. Under the current ownership of Middle West Partnerships, the shop remains on the ground floor; on the second floor is a sprawling workshop, which includes 80,000 original moulds and over 40,000 colour pencil sketches. Many of the jewellers have been there at least since the 1970s and still display a

reverence for the technique and legacy of this eponymous House and how the pieces are being reimagined for the modern day.

I was fortunate to interview Hope Alswang in 2013. The then director of the Norton Museum of Art in Palm Beach spoke to me regarding the David Webb retrospective, David Webb: Society Jewels. The exhibition, which ran from January through April 2014, showcased 80 pieces from the Webb archives and private collectors. "Webb captured the cultural revolution of the later '60s and

< 18K gold and platinum Paisley bracelet decorated with green and light blue enamel and set with cabochon rubies, emeralds and sapphires, and brilliant-cut diamonds, by David Webb, circa 1960s. Photograph courtesy of David Webb
ᐁ Verdura gold, yellow diamond, blue and green enamel 'Lotus Leaves' necklace, 1964. © Verdura
ᐳ Verdura sapphire, ruby, enamel and gold 'Frog' brooch, 1962. Originally from the collection of Mrs. William (Babe) Paley. © Verdura

'70s," Alswang explained. "I see 1968 as his turning point, when all of his major influences came into play, his travels and mixing elements of distant lands. His passion for exoticism and recapturing the Art Deco movement for which he had a true affinity, always was interpreted

with his distinctive wit and very unique and bold aesthetic." She continued: "He looked at styles of the '60s and translated this 'street style' into high-end luxury in a freewheeling, playful, stylised way that said 'I want to be seen!' "

Higgs mentions the important jewels of the '60s: "the animal cuffs in enamel and hardstones with gold and diamond heads and cabochon gemstone eyes, his paisley motif nod to Moghul Indian

jewellery, carved beads that spoke to his client's ideology of buying for herself – brave outspoken jewellery that was in keeping with the feminist wave and the sexual revolution. Think Gloria Steinem and Helen Gurley Brown."

Although the looks changed, the bold femininity remained throughout the early '70s. (See Chapter 9 for his designs for Jackie Kennedy and other famous women.)

During the '60s, Fulco di Verdura too took on a more inventively casual approach towards jewellery that could be worn for day and also for evening. His fascination with fruits and flowers continued to blossom into pieces that featured vibrantly coloured cabochons against three-dimensional gold, from lilies of the valley to pomegranates.

Ward Landrigan, who bought Verdura in 1999, notes: "Fulco had an uncanny ability to adapt his designs to each style or decade he was designing in, always within an aesthetic that was very Verdura. Throughout the '60s, he also took a more relaxed, alternative approach to jewellery – but then again he always was one step ahead, once turning seashells he purchased at the Museum of Natural History into works of fine jewellery art with precious gemstones." He also kept

his society clientele – and continued to design pieces for the women that Truman Capote dubbed 'The Swans' (see Chapter 4). "Two of these clients were Babe Paley, who was beautiful and his muse, and Slim Keith, who was also a dear friend," Landrigan reports. "She was one of the chicest women around during the time period in which he designed for her."

Verdura also dove into the world of semi-precious gemstones and created masterful pieces with turquoise, rose quartz, hardstones and translucent tourmalines, kunzite, pink topaz, aquamarine and amethyst. All were part of his arsenal, sometimes mixed together, other times standing on their own in statement pieces with enamel and diamond accents. His sense of

artistic composition could be seen in coral seashells wrapped in gold, and clams with sapphires, brooches featuring small creatures he brought to life, enamel green frogs with a reprise of Roman decorative motifs, cherubs (putti) riding snails of enamel, gold and rubies. Interestingly, he was offered a position similar to Schlumberger at Tiffany & Co., for which he would have creative licence and a permanent showcase – the window on Fifth Avenue. However flattered, he turned the offer down, working on his own for so many years, as he didn't feel he belonged in a corporate environment.

On a personal note, my mom (who was in her mid-to-late 20s during this decade) took trips over to London to buy her clothes. She got her hair cut at Vidal Sassoon and also wore wild print dresses from Pucci in Florence and a few 'mod' Space-Age dresses from Courrèges in Paris. Her pieces of jewellery were primarily those that my dad bought her,

some of which included brooches from Van Cleef & Arpels; witty animal cuffs and an Asian-inspired sautoir from David Webb; a Cartier jade, onyx and diamond clip brooch from the Art Deco period; and a perfectly matched strand of luminous Tiffany pearls. She often mixed the pieces from the different Houses together, and she had personal style in spades.

Like my mother, in the '60s women opted for personal style, which eventually led them to mix and mingle the works of different creators, as individual taste became predominant over the status and grandeur of renowned Houses. This resulted in more radical changes, as the last two years of the decade saw even more cultural and social influences. The same holds true in current times as individuality continues to play a major role in the purchase of vintage jewellery.

And the beat goes on...

< 'Lion's Paw' brooch, natural scallop shell, sapphire, diamond and gold, by Verdura. Commissioned by the Prince de Boncampagni. This piece was originally designed in 1942 and displays Verdura's creativity for found objects, which was seen throughout his career. © Verdura

∨ Diamond, sapphire, turquoise, emerald, platinum and gold 'Snake' brooch, 1967. © Verdura

And The Beat Goes On
The 1960s part 2

As the decade went on, American boys kept marching off to Vietnam. Protests and rallies against the war raged on college campuses throughout the USA. Martin Luther King Jr. and Bobby Kennedy were assassinated. The music icons of the day in the UK and USA wrote songs that captured the attitude of the times. The American youth continued to influence fashion and the term youthquake evolved into what was known as the anti-establishment counterculture, or 'hippies'. The Summer of Love in 1967 summed up the feeling of the movement and brought between 75,000 and 100,000 young Americans to Haight-Ashbury in San Francisco to protest the Vietnam War and materialism. They indulged in free love and drugs, tested alternative religions, and searched for some sort of meaning in what was happening around them.

As far as fashion, the hippies wore second-hand clothes, psychedelic prints, caftans and other ethnic dress, which influenced the designers of the day. The best example of this was Giorgio di Sant'

< Ali MacGraw, 1969 © Ullstein Bild Dtl. / ullstein bild via Getty Images
V Van Cleef & Arpels gold 'Alhambra' necklace. © Sotheby's

Angelo's high-end, stylised hippie chic. In Paris and London, the movement to more cross-cultural dressing and vivid prints took hold.

Says Adam Patrick of A La Vieille Russie: "The mod look was merged with the joyful, bright colours of hippie flower-power psychedelia, resulting in the emergence of beads, body paint and flowers adorning women's hair. This was the first time there was such diversity of cultures and styles in fashion and this impacted jewellery designers."

The jewellery became more and more relaxed, designed primarily in yellow gold, and inspired the movement towards more individualistic pieces that could go anwhere.

In 1968, Van Cleef & Arpels introduced the all-gold 'Alhambra' necklace for a more casual daytime approach to jewellery. Jacques was reported to have said: "To be lucky, you must believe in luck." The original version of the necklace featured 20 gold clovers stationed on a long chain. It would go on to be one of the most popular pieces in the early '70s, featuring different ornamental stones (see Chapter 9).

Artist jewellers continued to be popular throughout the USA and Europe, in particular Andrew Grima, Arthur King and Gilbert Albert. The Maisons didn't want to miss out, and so, as Kimberly Klosterman explains: "To battle these bold and interesting competitors, Cartier New York began to bring in interesting talent for artist exhibitions. The Kenton Corporation – a luxury company that

already included Kaplan Furs, Kenneth Jay Lane and Valentino – added the New York branch of Cartier to its holdings. In late November 1968, CEO Robert Kenmore, along with his stylish French wife Rosemary (formerly a gemmologist for Van Cleef & Arpels), sought to bring the well-known jewellery establishment into the modern era."

She continues: "In a few weeks, they found Michael Thomas, who had been a VP of merchandising for Neiman Marcus. It was no secret that the last 10 years or so at Cartier had been lacklustre, and it was the vision of President Michael Thomas that gave the firm a fresh and accessible new direction. The first show began in October 1969 with Roger Lucas, whose bold, over-the top designs were inspired by the Moon-landing, the sea, and geometry. An artist-jeweller from Montreal, Lucas learned the trade from an early age in his father's prestigious store, Gabriel Lucas. At age 21, he had become head of Cartier's workshop in Monte Carlo. Twelve years later, he would find himself selling to Chaumet; Piaget; and Shreve, Crump and Lowe, and opening a one man show at Cartier."

Klosterman then talks about Dinh Van.

"He originally began as a bench jeweller at Cartier Paris in 1955, was inspired by ready-to-wear and quit his job to open a workshop in 1965. His designs were sleek, elegant and simplistic. Made in polished gold and silver, his work was meant to be worn every day by everyone."

When the Kenton Corporation took over Cartier New York, they rehired him as part of their goal to expand the luxury goods conglomerate to multiple shopping malls, while still appealing to top-tier clients. And it worked." Lucas, Van and the young and creative genius Aldo Cipullo all brought the New York branch of Cartier back to life.

Astrology influenced jewellery, from the major Houses to independent designers, beginning in the 1960s and continuing in the '70s, when the trend exploded. Tiffany & Co. designed substantial, highly textured gold signet-style rings with raised zodiacs on the front, and pendants with astrological imagery on the front and glyphs on the reverse. Paul Vincze, a sculptor and medallist, brought his medium to zodiac motifs.

"When Vincze's pendants move, the elements on them seem to come to life, tricking the eye with a rich visual that mimics a three-dimensional sculpture," says Susan Cohen of Circa 1700. David Webb also dabbled in two-tone platinum and gold textural zodiac glyphs. In the following decade, more and more established Houses would go on to create their own astrological designs in different incarnations.

The last year of the decade proved to be one of the most inspirational years in jewellery. In 1969, three events made the news and captured the public imagination: on 21 July, watched by people around the world, the Commander of Apollo 11, Neil Armstrong, was the first man to walk on the Moon; and from 15-18 August, about 400,000 hippies and beatniks gathered for the Woodstock Music Festival. Both historic occasions influenced designers in the USA and abroad.

And then there was Cartier's most successful jewellery design hitting the stores at the height of the era that promoted 'Make Love Not War'. Aldo Cipullo's most iconic piece, the 'Love' bracelet, was perfectly in tune with the ethos of the late sixties, as well as the more simplistic looks of the time period.

The 'Love' Bracelet

In 1967, in the middle of the night, after a heartbreaking end to a relationship, Aldo Cipullo developed the idea for one of the most popular pieces of jewellery that has lived on for decades. The 'Love' bracelet goes on the wrist in two parts and is then secured by a small locking screwdriver. Also a unisex piece, it was ahead of its time and intended to be worn by both men and women. Renato Cipullo notes: "Aldo was inspired by ancient cultures and legends, including the medieval chastity belt. For Aldo, the bracelet stood for security as represented by the screwdriver that locked the piece together. By doing so, it also meant a lifetime of enduring commitment and everlasting love."

When Cipullo created the 'Love' bracelet, I doubt he had a clue that all these years later, women would not only still be wearing and coveting them but also stacking them with updates of the original bracelet, modern designer pieces, vintage and antique cuffs, bangles and flexible styles. He also didn't have to consider beepers going off at airport security lines or trying to explain to a guard who doesn't know what the 'Love' bracelet is, "Sorry but I really can't take it off", only to receive a full body search.

Cipullo's iconic piece has been seen on many A-list wrists over the decades and has also made it to the silver screen, with

V Cartier 'Love' bracelet, by Aldo Cipullo, circa 1970 © Sotheby's

Elizabeth Taylor wearing it in *XY and Zee* and Ali McGraw wearing hers from her first husband, the famous producer Robert Evans, in *The Getaway*.

With the continuing popularity of the original, over the years, Cartier has expanded the 'Love' range, which now includes a collection of rings, earrings, cufflinks and multiple versions of the bracelet with diamonds and coloured gemstones in pink, yellow and white gold.

Born in Naples in 1935, Cipullo grew up in Rome, the oldest of five children. His father owned a costume jewellery business. "After school, he would send Aldo out with a bag full of jewellery to sell," says Renato Cipullo, Aldo's brother who worked with him in New York and also became a designer in his own right.

Obsessed with all things American, Aldo was determined to move to the United States, and arrived there in 1959. He was hired for his first job by David Webb, eventually moving to Tiffany & Co. to work with Gene Moore, and be part of Tiffany's stable of young designers, including Donald Claflin. Cipullo came up with the concept of the 'Love' bracelet in 1967. "Aldo offered the bracelet to Tiffany & Co. but it was turned down and, in 1969, when his contract was up, he left and went and offered it to Michael Thomas, president of Cartier New York," Renato explains.

Thomas had the vision to see the potential and ingenuity of the design, the story behind it and a marketing plan that would launch the bracelet into the most successful piece in Cartier's history. His idea was to gift twin bracelets to the most influential couples he knew, including Liz Taylor and Richard Burton, Sophia Loren and Carlo Ponti and The Duke and Duchess of Windsor, who were just some of the famous couples who propelled the bracelet into celebrity status. Ali MacGraw,

whose star started to rise in the late 1960s, also owned one of the first bracelets. It was given to her by her then husband Robert Evans. She can be seen wearing it in the 1972 film *The Getaway*, starring alongside Steve McQueen, who she went on to marry after her divorce from Evans.

The design spurred other pieces that spoke of Aldo Cipullo's passion for the romance of the past mixed with the hardware elements with which his jewellery came to be synonymous. Cipullo became one of Cartier New York's most recognisable talents and his designs would become *the* jewellery to own in the 1970s; and they are still sought after by collectors from all demographics. Cipullo was the only designer who was allowed to sign his pieces for Cartier.

The Moon landing and space exploration provided inspiration for jewellery in designs that included Sputnik-shaped pieces, stars, rockets, craters and man-on-the-Moon imagery.

Lee Siegelson notes: "The Apollo 11 Moon landing in 1969 had a profound influence on design, inspiring a fascination with space exploration. The period was defined by the juxtaposition of tradition and futurism, which reflected the spirit of the jewellery surrounding the end of this decade and the beginning of the next."

< 18K gold and ruby 'Apollo' earrings, by Ilias Lalaounis, 1969. Courtesy of LALAoUNIS

V Jackie O, wearing her 'Moon-landing' earrings, celebrates her 40th birthday with husband Aristotle Onassis. © CSU Archives/Everett Collection/Bridgeman Images

Perhaps the most famed jewel that was indicative of the time and inspired by space exploration was Ilias Lalaounis's pair of "Apollo" earrings. Commissioned as a 40th birthday present for Jackie Kennedy Onassis by her second husband Aristotle Onassis, the dangling, tactile, hand-textured 18K gold spheres are meant to evoke the Moon. Demetra Lalaounis, one of Ilias' daughters and President of the company, explains: "Aristotle Onassis asked my father if he could design something for Jackie to commemorate the landing on the Moon and mark this historic event. My father chose to design a pair of earrings that he named the 'Apollo' earrings. The main part is a sphere representing the Moon, in hand-hammered gold with ruby accents. The top part of the earrings, which serves as the clip, is shaped as an orbit, and in-between the sphere and the clip are four identical motifs in the abstract shape of the command module (CM) of the spacecraft, called 'Columbia'. The subsequent designs for the 50th anniversary of the Moon landing were made in 18k gold with diamonds."

Susan Cohen was lucky enough to find two pendants that related to the Moon landing. "One was a vintage Man-on-the-Moon enamel 14K charm that was created to commemorate Neil Armstrong's famous first steps on the Moon. For those watching / listening in on this lunar landing – what a time of wonderment and hope that must have been," says Cohen. The other pendant she found "was more tongue-in-cheek: a gold man on the Moon with a rocket in his mouth, circa 1960s".

Jessica Sitko, partner with her husband in Trademark Antiques, scours the market for pieces from a vast range of periods. One of her finds was a vintage 14K gold pendant depicting the Apollo 11 Moon landing. On the reverse is written: "Armstrong-Aldrin-Collins; Apollo XI July 20, 1969; That's one small step for a man, one giant leap for mankind."

While these types of pieces that celebrated certain events have become more scarce, it is still feasible to score them by contacting different dealers, describing what you are looking for and asking them to search for you; eventually, you might get lucky either with a specific piece or a similar one.

As we leave the turbulent 1960s, we enter a new decade with a rocky start. The jewellery of the 1970s was, at first,

an extension of what had been been created in the '60s. Designers then began developing their aesthetics, gaining a cult following as they mirrored the aspects of a new time period.

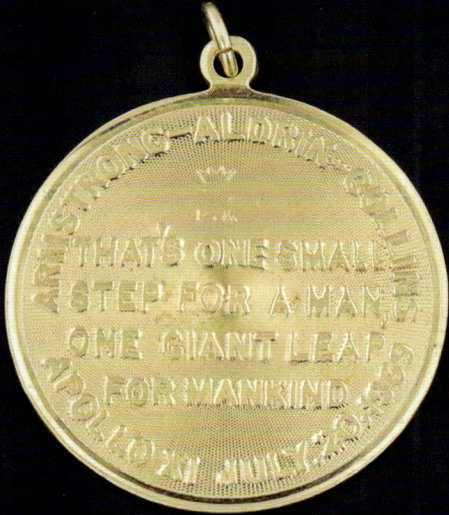

What's Going On
The 1970s

At the beginning of the '70s, the USA was still protesting against the Vietnam War as Marvin Gaye's hit song *What's Going On* climbed the charts in 1971 with lyrics telling us that war was not the answer.

Other cultural, political and social 'goings on' were the Watergate scandal, the sexual revolution and second-wave feminism, which originated in the '60s, the start of disco music and clubs. We also saw different modes of dress: ethnic, streamlined and man-made materials that looked good under flashing neon lights and mirror balls at the clubs both in the USA and Europe.

By 1973 the war had finally ended and the American writer Eric Jong's 1973 novel *Fear of Flying* was a #1 best seller internationally, catching on with feminists and those who were becoming sexually liberated. Suburban housewives, who had married young and were starting to feel the effects of growing into different people, also took note, resulting in a wave of divorce that we hadn't witnessed before.

My mother was one of those women. In 1973, at the age of 35, she and my dad divorced. They were the first divorced couple I knew of, besides hearing about Sonny and Cher. Mom gave up her budding career at 21 years old to become a middle-class, country club housewife and mother to three children.

Then, after the divorce, she once again entered the workforce in 1974 as a senior vice president of a large ready-to-wear company. Although she wore more of the styles coming out of London in the '60s, in the '70s she chose the American designers: Diane Von Furstenberg, Anne Klein and Calvin Klein for work, and Halston for going out in the evenings. On weekends, while dating a handsome French-Canadian artist, she wore peasant blouses, bell-bottom jeans and maxi dresses. This was basically the same type of clothes that I wore while navigating junior high school into high school – sometimes she even borrowed my clothes and looked better in them than me. She also changed her hair to a wash-and-wear shag, and her jewellery to what would become some of the major pieces in the 1970s.

Like many of my peers, by the time I was 15 and in 10th grade, I got fake ID. I loved to dance, and the pulsating sounds of the disco music drew me to the clubs in our hometown, 20 minutes from Manhattan. My last year in high school in 1977, the year *Saturday Night Fever* was released, I was 'clubbing' in the city.

∨ Van Cleef & Arpels gold 'Manchette' cuff bracelets, circa 1977. This design was famously worn by Jackie Onassis in the early '70s. Collection of Kimberly Klosterman, Photography by Tony Walsh, Courtesy of the Cincinnati Art Museum
> Bulgari convertible sautoir-brooch in gold with rhodonite, rubellites, sapphires and diamonds, circa 1972. © Bulgari Heritage Collection. Photo: Barrella – Studio Orizzonte Gallery

Then, in Boston discos during college, I wore the requisite Lycra slinky dress, tube tops, halter- and wrap dresses and yellow-gold jewellery to complement them.

In the USA, the jewellery went hand in hand with what was happening at the time. The '70s were a time of social upheaval and strong style statements, and the jewellery trends of the era were just as meaningful and bold. Aldo Cipullo and David Webb flourished. The established jewellery Maisons of Van Cleef & Arpels, Bulgari and Cartier were savvy enough to understand the cultural changes that were taking place and astutely introduced styles that had mass appeal and perfectly bejewelled the fashions of the times. The decade wasn't ablaze with diamonds, rather it was defined by sculpted and textured metal.

Siegelson cites Jackie O's 'Crater' cuffs by Van Cleef & Arpels. These cuffs didn't match perfectly but instead were created as a set of similar bracelets that

were textured in the brutalist sensibility, representing the surface of the Moon. They were designed in 1973, four years after the Moon landing, as the early years of the '70s were still very inspired by space travel.

New names like Elsa Peretti took the jewellery scene by storm, joining the ranks of Tiffany & Co.'s designers.

The iconic '70s jewellery pieces were not only revolutionary, they were also evolutionary. Many are still produced today. Thanks to the new generation, who are seeing these designs for the very first time, there is both a revival of the vintage and the emergence of new incarnations. The history of these pieces, the celebrity factor then and now, and the wearable versatility have rendered the jewellery of the 1970s as collectible and coveted today as they were when they were first introduced.

The Jewellery that Topped the '70s Charts

Aldo Cipullo's 'Love' bracelet was still going strong – it has also come to mean everlasting chic. Both celebrities and women of all demographics are still head over heels with the original style as well as the myriad variations that have been launched since.

In 1971 Cipullo designed another iconic piece: the 'Nail' bracelet, which was renamed 'Juste un Clou' (Just a Nail) when it was rereleased in 2012. The design was inspired by a book Cipullo was reading about Christianity and self-sacrifice as the greatest gift of love. His penchant for hardware and industrial design mixed with romanticism and storytelling resulted in a bracelet in which a nail is wrapped around the wrist, with the head on one end and the sharp point on the other. In advertisements, Cartier New York played up the bracelet's connotations of love, and it was another huge success. Nail jabot pins and cufflinks were added to the unisex bracelet, capturing the essence of the classic chic and gritty edginess of New York City.

According to Renato Cipullo: "Aldo particularly enjoyed drawing inspiration from everyday items and his surroundings so it's no surprise he was influenced by our trips to the hardware store or art that he saw while walking around the city." The minimalism and mechanics of nuts, bolts and screws figured into his designs were both elegant yet edgy, which appealed and resonated with more youthful and sophisticated generations.

According to the Cincinnati Art Museum, in 1971, Cipullo introduced the Hamsa pendant, a more craftsy yet stylised design. Based on an amulet popular in North Africa and the Middle East that was believed to protect the wearer against evil, it features an eye-shaped opening (suggesting the Evil Eye often seen in the traditional Hamsa) in the palm of a flat, stylised hand. Renato Cipullo explains: "Aldo named

this piece the 'Hand of the Heart'. He was interested in mysticism and the symbology behind it and this type of hand is represented in many cultures." He continues: "Aldo was a very kind and loving person, so it seems natural he would continuously look towards imagery that would reflect his faith in love, connections and protection." The pendant was worn by Ellen Burstyn in the 1973 film *The Exorcist,* along with a 'Love' bracelet; Aldo Cipullo was listed in the credits as jewellery designer, which once again propelled him into the spotlight.

In his next collection, Cipullo was inspired by both New York's graffiti and Robert Indiana's iconic LOVE sculpture, which stood on 6th Avenue. He designed a series of brooches and pendants with the word "love" spelled out in capital letters. These appeared in 1972 and 1973, and were featured in Cartier New York's advertisements, which read: "Cartier is when you want to say thank you for loving me" and "Cartier: Because you Love her". Brooches were horizontal, like badges, with the 'O' replaced by a carved coral heart or by a screwhead, drawing attention to the roundness of the letter.

Says Susan Cohen of Circa 1700: "I have a strong affinity for Cipullo and the

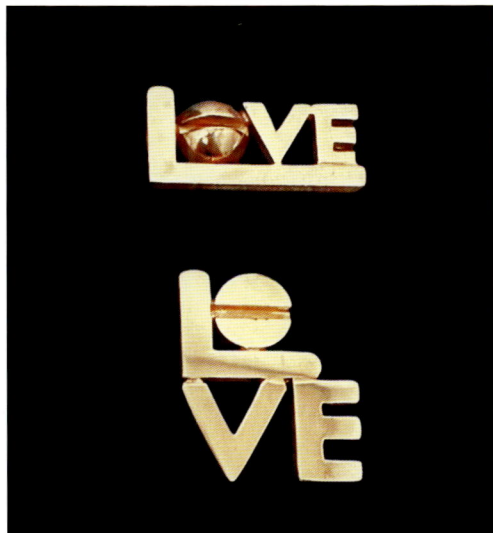

way he played with mechanical elements to reinvent timeless talismans while rooting them in an era where war was in the headlines, but the world yearned for peace and love. He captured this dichotomy perfectly. Whenever I can find a Cipullo piece, I snap it up and oftentimes I keep them for myself, selling off only a few of the pieces I have found."

Other designs for Cartier New York were drawn from poker and backgammon. "Aldo brought brooches back in a playful and fashionable way – pins in yellow gold in the shape of the suits of playing cards that were three-dimensional: hearts, clubs, spades and diamonds." Renato Cipullo offers: "During that period, Aldo kept a deck of cards on his coffee table and it was a time when card games and backgammon games were very popular social activities." The backgammon jewellery was promoted as the Cartier Game.

"It was an exhilarating time in New York City," Renato continues. "Working with my brother, I met a whole world of creative people in fashion, architecture, other jewellers and was a guest at Studio 54, thanks to Aldo and his friendship with Steve Rubell. We socialised with Andy Warhol, Margaux Hemingway and Grace Jones, among so many others, and it was as exciting as you'd expect. Aldo was always a big part of the scene there and wherever he went. He had movie star good looks and a charismatic personality, along with the talent to keep evolving with the times."

Cipullo understood this disco nightlife and created pieces that worked under the flashing neon lights as well as pieces

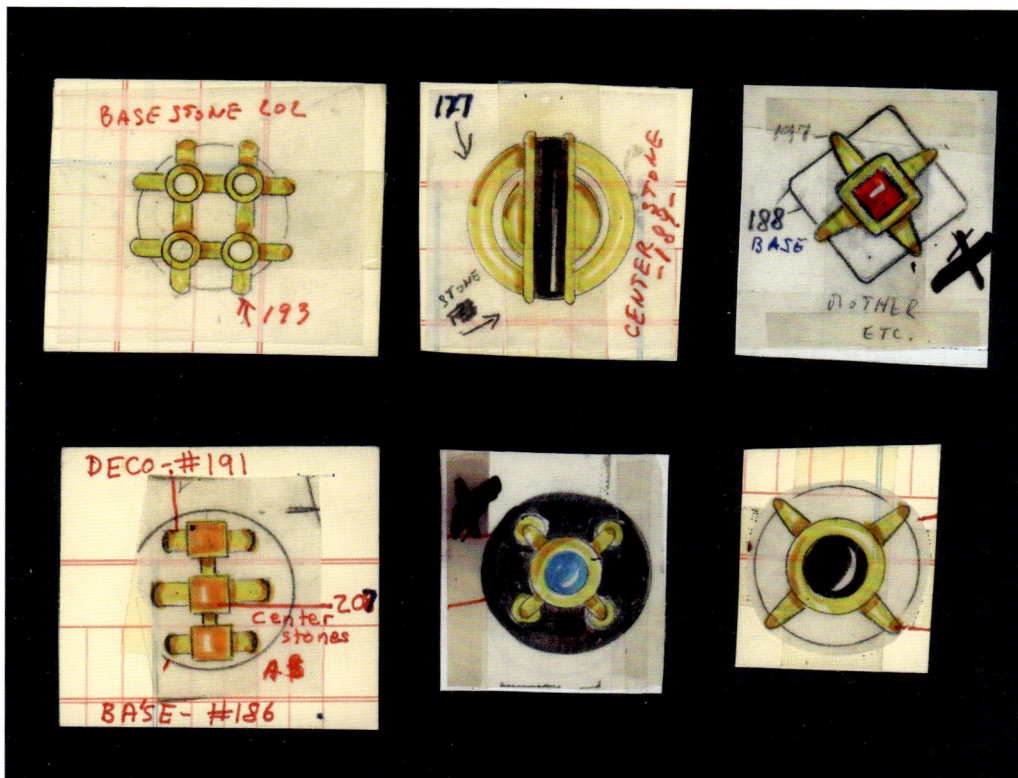

a woman could wear to work. He created a series of stud earrings that could be worn for any occasion, that were modern yet had beautiful colours of hardstone and gems, framed in Art Deco-inspired geometrical round shapes.

The last designs he made for Cartier were a mix of 18K yellow gold and hardstone links of onyx, malachite, tiger's eye and other stones for necklaces and bracelets. These were his most sophisticated pieces, yet still could be worn in the way all his pieces could – with a nonchalant confidence.

According to Renato: "Aldo always had a separate studio next door to his apartment, he loved the autonomy and could work much more freely that way. His designs were commissioned rather than Aldo being employed by Cartier; therefore, he also had the ability to work on his own designs and custom pieces." In 1974, when Cartier New York was merged back together with London and Paris into a global company, Aldo Cipullo went out on his own and designed private commissions as well as collections under his name until his untimely death in 1984.

Renato continues: "When Aldo passed away at the very young age of 62, Cartier

< 'Alhambra' necklace, 1970. Yellow gold, malachite. Van Cleef & Arpels Collection. © Van Cleef & Arpels SA
> 'Hutton' ring from the Twilight Collection, carved rock crystal, brilliant-cut diamonds, 18K white gold and platinum, by David Webb. Photograph courtesy of David Webb
>∨ 'Twist' cuff from the Twilight Collection, carved rock crystal, brilliant-cut diamonds, 18K white gold and platinum, by David Webb, circa 1970s. Photograph courtesy of David Webb

purchased the rights from our father, Aldo's executor, to own the pieces for Cartier."

Like the Cartier 'Love' bracelet, the Van Cleef & Arpels 'Alhambra' long necklace was first introduced in the late 1960s (see Chapter 9) but became one of the most popular jewels of the 1970s. Established as the legendary Maison's icon of luck, the collection evolved to include hardstones set into the clover stations: malachite, tiger's eye, lapis lazuli, onyx, coral and turquoise. This casual style of necklace was exactly what women desired at the time and still covet today. Princess Grace wore her 'Alhambra' necklaces throughout the '70s. The collection has constantly been renewed over the years in multiple variations of motif sizes and materials. Long and short necklaces, earrings, rings, bracelets and watches reproduce the motifs in gold, hardstones and precious gems.

David Webb was another designer who continued to evolve and make his mark again in the '70s. Says Levi Higgs: "For David Webb, the 1970s was more linear, geometric with enamel work and bold graphic styles." Webb said at the time: "rock crystal is the only white alternative to diamonds" and he created cuffs and rings in rock crystal with precious stone and enamel accents. "The animals so prevalent in the '60s and other three-dimensional creatures gave way to colour in a Mondrian sense," says Higgs. "Also a fan of the disco era, he created the '70s version of long sautoirs that would be the perfect necklace to go out to a club to wear with the fashions of the day."

< 'Lex' necklace, black enamel triptych links with brilliant-cut diamonds, polished 18K gold and platinum, by David Webb, circa 1970s. Photograph courtesy of David Webb

V 'Scroll' earrings, carved jade, brilliant-cut diamonds, black enamel, 18K gold and platinum, by David Webb, circa 1970s. Photograph courtesy of David Webb

'Monete' jewels would become some of the most emblematic Bulgari pieces of the 1970s – appealing both to existing and new clients.

The 'it' actresses of the day – Susan Sarandon, Candice Bergen and Jane Fonda, among others – all owned the curb chain necklace with the ancient coins bezelled in 18K gold. The mounted antique coins speak to a long standing

You can find vintage pieces on the market but, as Higgs explains: "We have people from the '70s still working in the factory and we are creating new pieces based on the same moulds and sketches and due to technological advances, we have learned to make a better fit, and a perfectly executed piece for a whole new generation of David Webb collectors."

After years of luxurious and glamorous gemstone and diamond jewellery, Bulgari, which was passed down from generation to generation, had found a way in the mid-'60s to create jewellery to wear every day that was still elegant. While the renowned House's 'Serpenti' collection continued to attract the attention of celebrities, socialites and collectors, it was the Monete collection that truly took on the '70s vibe and caused a sensation.

> 'Serpenti' watch. © Bulgari Heritage Collection.
Photo: Barrella – Studio Orizzonte Gallery
∨ 'Serpenti' necklace in gold with white enamel, Bulgari,
circa 1970. © Bulgari Heritage Collection. Photo: Barrella –
Studio Orizzonte Gallery

tradition in jewellery dating back to Ancient Rome. In all the 'Monete' pieces, the authentic coins are preserved unaltered: the mountings follow their contours. Each bezel setting is engraved on the back in Italian with the name of the emperor who is featured on the coin, the dates they were in power and the type of coin. Bulgari's original ancient coins were first seen adorning precious objects such as cigarette cases in the 1930s, but it was Nicola Bulgari, an avid collector of these coins since childhood, who revisited this approach and started to mount them into jewels from the mid-'60s on. All vintage '70s 'Monete' pieces are extremely collectible and wearable, especially if they are in good condition.

Talking about classics that retained their style and cool allure that speak to all generations, I can still immediately picture the undulated shapes of Elsa Peretti's designs. Organic and sculptured at the same time, they effortlessly take on the personality of the wearer. Her pieces have become icons in their own right, as powerful and enduring as the woman who designed them. Amid the feminist movement and disco nights, Peretti was a visionary: bold and brave enough to design jewellery for women like herself – strong, independent working women – who wanted to look confident while climbing the corporate ladder *and* feel sexy on the dance floor.

She was also savvy enough to understand the cultural shifts and changes that were taking place and created pieces that reflected the times. Her sensual designs, with their sense of poetry, movement and minimalism, defined a decade and continue to inspire women today. Peretti also had an affinity for sterling silver and created pieces that spoke of luxury at accessible price points.

Her bone cuff is perhaps the most recognisable piece of her arsenal of jewellery for Tiffany & Co.; polished, yet with a primitive silhouette that seamlessly hugged the contours of the wrist. It was the piece of jewellery that all mothers I knew were wearing, and all the daughters like me wanted. My mother owned the more exaggerated style of the cuff and I was presented my own first classic bone cuff for my 'sweet sixteen', and then another when I went off to college. One for each wrist. And how happy that made me to be wearing the cuff that was owned by celebrities such as Sophia Loren and Liza Minnelli, not to mention style icon, Diana Vreeland. It still graces the wrists of many style-setting actresses, such as Rosamund Pike, Rachel Weisz and Naomi Watts. These leading ladies have worn this cuff to various red carpet events in recent years – proof that Peretti's original pieces continue to have a modern and timely appeal.

Peretti was educated in both Italy and Switzerland and started her career

V Gold 'Scorpion' necklace, Elsa Peretti, circa 1979.
Collection of Kimberly Klosterman, Photography by Tony
Walsh, Courtesy of the Cincinnati Art Museum

in the USA as a model. When she began to design her first pieces of jewellery, Giorgio di Sant' Angelo commissioned styles for a fashion show, which were an instant success. Around this time she met Halston, who became a long-time friend and collaborator. She designed pieces for him before being hired by Tiffany & Co. in 1974, when the renowned jewellery Maison introduced the Elsa Peretti collection. Her style was inspired by abstract interpretations of the organic forms. Other recognisable pieces for Tiffany & Co. include the 'Bottle', 'Bean' and 'Open Heart' pendants and her 'Diamonds by the Yard' necklaces, as well as the much-coveted 'Snake' and 'Scorpion' necklaces. Being born at the beginning of November, I was lucky enough to be presented with the brilliantly executed 'Scorpion' necklace, which came out in 1979, when I was in college.

In 2013, Peretti briefly considered retiring and taking her copyrighted designs. But she had a change of heart and signed a new 20-year contract with Tiffany. The spring of 2016 heralded the launch of @elsaperettiofficial on social media, which offers a personal peek into the designer's thought processes and life. Her Instagram feed offers sketches and snippets of her inspirations and quotes, and posts of her most

legendary jewels. It was a brilliant move to create awareness and introduce new generations to the wildly creative Peretti, whose imagination broke down boundaries, and who designed some of the top sellers of all time. She passed away at the age of 80 in 2021.

a huge cultural trend that started in the '60s and reached the height of its popularity in the '70s, and both Paris and New York's established Maisons, such as Cartier, Van Cleef & Arpels and Tiffany & Co., all created jewellery in the theme.

Van Cleef & Arpels had been interested in outer space since its inception and has been creating astrology-inspired jewellery since 1953. The 1970s styles were created as round medals in yellow gold or set with ornamental stones with braided edges and gemstones set in the eyes of some of the astrological signs.

Susan Cohen, from Circa 1700, explains: "The '70s were a time in which zodiac talismans took centre stage. Crafted to be big and bold, these pieces made a definite statement about their wearer. Each House had their own take. A treasure hunt that is definitely worth the effort are Cartier's 'Zodiac' rings, a unique twist in their design and makes for a whimsical addition to any ring stack. Cartier also built on their 'Zodiac' rings by crafting a number of large pendants that mirrored the rings' design."

Sign of the Times

The '70s was a period when people were looking for meaning after all the challenges and upheaval faced from the '60s through the early part of the decade. In addition to feeling free and letting go on the dance floor, to exploring sexuality, and the search to find oneself in different types of group therapy, it was a generation that also looked to astrology for direction and guidance. Zodiacs were

> Aries pendant, circa 1974. Yellow gold, emerald, malachite, diamond. Van Cleef & Arpels Collection. © Van Cleef & Arpels SA.

VV 18K gold 'Zodiac' rings, Cartier New York, circa 1970s. Courtesy of Circa 1700

She continues: "Paul Vincze continued to design astrological pendants. There is something truly evocative about his work. Being a sculptor and medallist, he brings to life the human form that is completely mesmerising to behold. It's as if the forms he has sculpted are moving as light strikes the gold – breathing life into these little masterpieces."

Chaumet crafted a two-tone brutalist design utilising yellow and white gold. The white-gold zodiac appears to pop out of the yellow-gold backdrop.

Tennis Anyone?

"My diamond bracelet, which fell off during a match at the US Open many years ago, became an iconic jewellery category with a life of its own," says tennis legend Chris Evert: "I wanted to look and feel feminine yet empowered while playing, so what many now know as a 'tennis bracelet' started out as a piece of daily armour to give me strength on the court."

Evert was engaged in a long rally during the 1978 US Open when her bezel-set diamond bracelet went flying across the court. She asked officials to stop the match until she found the bracelet. From then on, the name became indelibly linked to the flexible diamond bracelets that had been known as 'eternity' or 'line' bracelets from the Art Deco period up until the time of *that* tennis match. Soon jewellers began receiving an onslaught of requests for 'tennis bracelets', which they began to produce in different cuts, carat weights, settings and metals.

According to Greg Kwiat, co-owner of Kwiat and Fred Leighton: "The diamond tennis bracelet remains as relevant now as ever, and is definitely a piece that's desired by our younger clientele. They want to wear jewellery that can make a style statement when worn

V Tennis bracelet, 18K gold and brilliant-cut diamonds.
© Sotheby's

alone or stacked. A look we have been seeing lately is the combining of two or three tennis bracelets to create a more impactful presence."

Vintage styles can be found from the 1970s through early '80s. But to obtain a vintage bracelet, be wary and ask dealers many questions as there are also styles that almost every jeweller and manufacturer has produced since then. If you go for new, Chris Evert partnered with contemporary designer Monica Rich Kosann, who was open to telling Evert's story and designing pieces that are inspired by the day of that 1978 match. Evert says: "When I first met Monica, I shared things I remembered about that day...the green court, the white lines, the dripping sweat, and my diamond bracelet.

She listened and incorporated all these distinct moments into the designs for our collection together. It is my hope that the pieces we created together become a woman's daily armour in every facet of her life to conquer the day ahead."

As we come to the end of the '70s, an era that was full of strife and life, there are many styles that collectors are still hankering for today. The meaning, ease of wear, and how the pieces fit in with modern-day jewellery have propelled them to become some of the most iconic pieces of all time.

The Last Days
of Disco/Working Girl
Early 1980s

The early '80s was a turning point in both music and in women's roles in the workforce – and the jewellery reflected both. Disco was on the way out; Studio 54 closed and other venues, which once spun the multiple artists of the popular pulsating beat, were now mixing fresh sounds of the new decade: electronic funk, house music and hip hop, while new wave and punk became equally popular.

The bold yellow gold that had glittered under the strobing disco lights was making its way from the dance floor into the boardroom as more and more women entered the workforce, tearing down barriers. Women realised they could be anything they wanted to be, going after the careers that best suited them, and they started having more disposable income to buy their own jewellery. It was the start of a trend that continued to grow stronger as we entered the 21st century, and even more so in recent years: designing and marketing to the self-purchasing woman.

V Gal Gadot, like many of the other stars during the 2024/25 awards season, brings vintage jewellery into modern times. She attends the Oscars wearing an archival vintage 18K gold and platinum necklace edged with 433 diamonds, designed in 1980 by Angela Cummings for Tiffany & Co. © John Salangsang/BEI/Shutterstock

> 'Parentesi' necklace, bangle and earrings in gold with diamonds, Bulgari, circa 1982. © Bulgari Heritage Collection. Photo: Barrella - Studio Orizzonte Gallery

The jewellery of the early '80s was bold, gutsy and statement-making, reflecting the confidence and the clothes that women were wearing to project professionalism. Giorgio Armani in Milan, Karl Lagerfeld for Chanel in Paris, Calvin Klein in New York, to name just a few designers, all provided structured trouser suits, blazers, below-the-knee skirts and coats that were menswear-inspired and powerful in tailoring but feminised for the professional woman.

Yellow gold continued as the popular metal choice, although it was often combined with other colour metals, stones or enamel, mostly in grey or black tones. Pieces were sculptural in clean-lined polished metals or organic with a nod to nature, but in more elegant, refined textures than we saw in the 1970s. Precious and semi-precious stones were incorporated into the designs both in the USA and Europe and featured cabochons and fancy propriety cuts that lapidaries produced for different designers and Houses. South Sea and cultured pearls saw a revival not seen since the 1950s and were once again at the height of fashion. They were often worn in graduating lengths in multiple strands or combined with large juicy stones.

Elsa Peretti continued to sell her iconic pieces and design well into the 1980s for women in varied careers, building on her most popular pieces. Part of Peretti's success was intuitively knowing what a wide demographic of women would want to wear. She elevated sterling silver, and also designed in 18K gold and other materials that appealed to women on multiple levels and for all times of the day or evening. To meet the growing demand of the new generation of career women who desired jewellery that would project strength yet were wearable and versatile pieces, Tiffany & Co. hired two more female designers: Paloma Picasso and Angela Cummings.

Paloma Picasso, the daughter of artist Pablo Picasso, was born in Vallauris, France, in 1949 and was named for the Spanish word for 'dove'. Her father featured the peace dove in many of his works. As a child, Paloma already displayed her creativity through drawings but it wasn't her dream to become the same type of artist as her father. After attending the University of Paris, she worked as a theatrical costume designer before turning to jewellery design in the late 1960s. Yves Saint Laurent was a friend and, after seeing her designs, he hired her to create costume jewellery. When Pablo Picasso died in 1973, Paloma paused her design career to help

organise her father's estate; she also acted in French films and then designed movie sets.

Finally she returned to jewellery design in the late 1970s to design for a Greek jewellery company. In 1980, the design director of Tiffany & Co., John Loring – who had known her since she was a teenager and was impressed by her talent – asked Paloma to join the company. As the daughter of two painters – her mother was Françoise Gilot – she was mesmerised by all of the different precious and semi-precious stones that she had access to at Tiffany, and included bold, daring mixes of colour and cuts in her designs.

In 1983, she created a collection that was a huge success. It was on target with the times and easier to manufacture than the intricate combinations of large stones and pearls. Drawing from urban street art on buildings and in the subways, which was thought of as vandalism in New York City, she set out to change the image of graffiti with her collection for the renowned company, and called it 'Paloma's Graffiti'. The imagery for hugs

and kisses featured prominently in this collection, in both gold and silver, as did squiggle brooches and doodles, as well as her iconic heart that forms an X at the bottom. Of the time, she explains: "In the '70s, people were starting to tag subways and walls, which had everyone outraged. I wanted to look at graffiti differently and try to make something positive out of it." And so she did. Says Kerri Orlando, jewellery specialist of Wilson's Estate Jewelry: "We're all familiar with the bold and chunky gold jewellery of the '80s brought on by a boom of there being more women in the workplace and in control of their own income. Paloma pushed that a little further and gave women a more expressive option. Although cities fought use of

< 18K gold large 'Squiggle' brooch, by Paloma Picasso
for Tiffany & Co., circa 1983. Courtesy of Wilson's Estate
Jewelry
<V 18K gold 'Graffiti love and kisses xo' charm pendant,
by Paloma Picasso for Tiffany & Co. Courtesy of Wilson's
Estate Jewelry
V 18K gold 'Graffiti X' earrings, by Paloma Picasso for
Tiffany & Co., circa 1980. Courtesy of Wilson's Estate
Jewelry

graffiti on municipal structures, she used
the essence and concept that mimicked
the art form as an influence for this
collection, with a lighter, more whimsical
touch to the pieces."

These styles best illustrate her
work from the early '80s and were a hit
with the executive woman, who was
purchasing her own jewels. Paloma
Picasso's designs for Tiffany & Co.
continue to evolve, producing successful
collections throughout the decades since
her first designs.

Born during World War II in Austria,
Angela Cummings relocated to the USA
with her family when she was three years
old. As a teenager, she went to Perugia in
Italy to study art and then on to Hanau,

> Gold necklace, by Angela Cummings for Tiffany & Co., 1981. © Sotheby's
∨ 18K gold, black jade and opal bangle, by Angela Cummings for Tiffany & Co., circa 1982–83. Courtesy of Macklowe Gallery

Germany, to learn jewellery design, where she graduated with a degree in goldsmithing and gemmology.

Cummings moved to New York and quickly joined the ranks of named designers at Tiffany & Co., working first under the guidance of Donald Claflin in 1968. Her collection 'Angela Cummings Exclusively for Tiffany & Co.' eventually launched for the legendary company in 1975.

The styles that she made popular in the early 1980s were polished gold pieces with geometric inlays of coral, wood, lapis lazuli, jade, onyx and mother-of-pearl. But her most striking designs were inspired by nature, including sea life, floral and wildlife motifs, and gave a nod to all types of botanicals in necklaces and bracelets. A 1982 *People* magazine article featured her iconic rose-petal demi-suite, as well as other 18K gold pieces she created for Tiffany & Co., including a spider's web necklace and elm leaf earrings.

When Cummings left Tiffany & Co. in 1984 to strike out on her own, she and her husband Bruce Cummings, another Tiffany & Co. alumni, opened a boutique inside Bergdorf Goodman; other major stores followed. Both her signed pieces for Tiffany & Co., created during the '70s and '80s, and her own brand collections remain highly recognisable and collectible to this day.

While the designers for Tiffany & Co. appealed to the customers who shopped on Manhattan's Fifth Avenue, SoHo (short for South of Houston Street) was abuzz with celebrities, fashion designers and international tourists, all visiting this mecca of painters, sculptors and performance artists... and Robert Lee Morris and his iconic shop Artwear. Morris first opened in 1978 on East 74th Street near the Madison Avenue's couture shops, but moved to where it would be more at home, surrounded by contemporary art galleries on the corner of West Broadway and Spring Street.

SoHo's transition from factories into artists' lofts and galleries began in the 1970s, but took off in the 1980s and fast became the international epicentre for the discovery of new artists and a shopping area that attracted global press and a who's who list of musicians, actors and actresses of the day. Artwear was one of the main attractions throughout the 1980s. Robert Lee Morris was dubbed the 'Father of New Artist Jewellery Designers' due to his inventive interpretations of sensually sculptural and often primitive and organic-inspired designs, and his featuring the work of some of the most innovative jewellers of the time in Artwear. These designers included, but were not limited to, Ted Muehling, Cara Croninger, Patricia Von Musulin and John Iverson. He also collaborated with some of the world's leading fashion designers from the 1980s onward.

A metalsmith and sculptor, unlike some of his contemporaries, Robert Lee Morris's work was not created in precious metals, but they landed on the cover of all the fashion magazines and appealed to a roster of clientele, who included Madonna, Cher, Bianca Jagger, Oprah Winfrey and Mariel Hemingway, to name just a few. This led to other shops, such as Saks Fifth Avenue purchasing his collections, his pieces being featured as museum exhibits, another Artwear store opening, and different licensees. But perhaps the most legendary time of his career was his collaboration with Donna Karan. They first met in 1983 when she was designing for Anne Klein, and they then went on to work together on her runway shows after Karan launched her own collection in 1985. She personified the working woman herself, and through

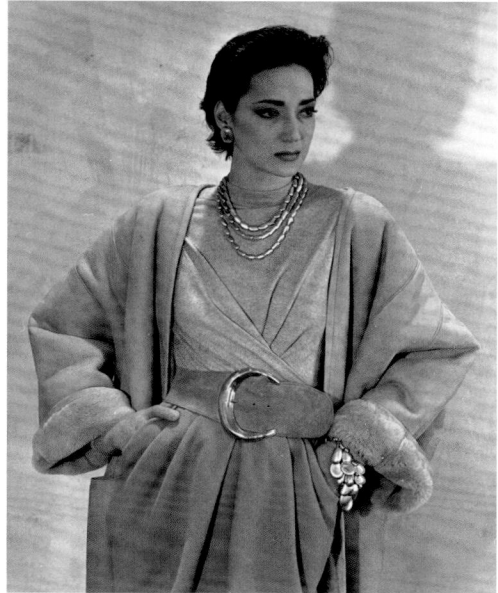

her designs and Morris' bold gold jewellery, the combination of the two became associated with what modern women wanted to own and wear. Morris designed 28 collections for Karan that continued until the early 1990s. He also worked with Calvin Klein and Michael Kors on their runway shows.

Born in Germany in 1947, he was a self-described army brat who moved around 23 times. After graduating in art and archeology from Beloit College, he founded an artist commune with friends from school and began making art from metalwork using hardware-store materials; the commune burnt down in the 1970s. Morris' work was discovered by Joan Sonnabend and Phyllis Rosen at a craft show at Putney School, Putney, Vermont. Sonnabend and Rosen were collectors of art jewellery and had just opened the Sculpture to Wear gallery at the Plaza hotel, carrying work by Pablo Picasso, Man Ray and Alexander Calder. They provided Morris with a one-man show in the lobby of the hotel, which won him recognition and sparked his rise to fame. It was when the store shut down that Morris searched around for a new home and found it in Artwear.

He was the recipient of the prestigious Coty Award in 1981 and his first CFDA Award in 1985. He was cited as being one of the most influential groundbreakers in the artist jewellery community, redefining how the medium was seen, merchandised and worn.

In the early '80s, New York designer Henry Dunay captured the attention of the US and European jewellery market. Linda Orlick, founder and CEO of Goldstein Communications, who helped launch Henry Dunay's career, explains: "I first met jewellery designer Henry Dunay in 1981. In his early years he became known for his faceted finish; he used 18.5 karat gold which gave his designs a distinctive look. He mixed smooth and textured finishes and also worked with braided elements at the time. Henry also had an incredible eye when it came to choosing pearls,

which were sold during the Lauren Bacall Collection auction at Bonham's New York in 2015. Gage was inspired by the ancient Roman and Renaissance periods and, in her wildly inventive take on bringing the past into the present, she combined antique coins, carved gemstones, 18th-century glass intaglios with baroque pearls, diamonds, and myriad beautiful coloured stones. Gage's designs were dramatic statement and conversation pieces and continued to be so throughout the '80s and well into the new millennium.

Bulgari continued to be a major player in the 1980s, producing pieces that were in keeping with the times once again, well suited to business attire, and also could take a woman from meetings to cocktails to dinner. The company expanded even further on the Monete collection and worked them into everything from a simple single necklace to a three-tier collar to multiple coins on one necklace. In the early '80s, Bulgari also introduced the Parentesi collection, which was perhaps the most desirable of this period. It focused on modular jewellery in clean silhouettes of chokers and suites of large earrings with matching bracelets. The choker also appeared in two-tone gold combinations or with stone inlays

precious and semi-precious stones. He never designed a piece of jewellery and then went searching for the right stone; he selected the one that spoke to him and that stone gave him a vision to design the piece. Henry also had an incredible eye for diamonds; he always had to have the best colour and clarity. He was called the Fabergé of his time; he created works of art using gold, platinum, diamonds, pearls, and semi-precious stones as his medium."

Dunay's success with this type of jewellery paved the way for relatively unknown emerging American fine-jewellery designers to become internationally recognised. He continued to design until the early part of the millennium.

Lauren Bacall was a collector of Elizabeth Gage's jewellery, some of

> 'Doppio Cuore' tubogas choker in steel and gold, Bulgari, 1984. © Bulgari Heritage Collection Photo: Barrella - Studio Orizzonte Gallery
V Gem-set and diamond bracelet, Marina B, 1980s. © Sotheby's

between the interlocking links. The double-heart collection was also popular during this time, particularly with bold, colourful cabochons set into the heart sections of the pieces or also in two-tone heart silhouettes within the designs of the pieces.

Marina B worked closely with her father Constantino Bulgari (the eldest son of the legendary House's founder Sotirio Bulgari) to learn the exacting techniques of jewellery design, and worked for the family business alongside her sister and cousins. After her father's death, she decided to break away to start her own jewellery company, with the condition imposed by her cousins in the family business that she not use the name Bulgari. She designed under the name Marina B, and throughout the '80s developed her own recognisable style.

One of the main concepts she worked with was interchangeable jewels – she designed earrings in which the gemstone drops could be changed out with other colours, and central stones could be swapped with other stones. Guy Bedarida, Chairman and Creative Director of the Marina B company since 2017, explains:

"The 1980s were a transformative period for women, as they embraced new careers (and new incomes). Marina's pieces were designed with these women in mind, and what she created was bought by the women who wore them, not by men as gifts. In light of this, she created many earrings that could transform, to provide her loyal customers with a plethora of options in a single piece and a greater

value." She also designed reversible pieces with a different front and back, which could be worn on either side. She often used black gold, onyx or black mother-of-pearl as the backdrop of her jewels to accentuate vibrant gemstones, diamonds and pearls. From her education in workshops at a young age, she learned different techniques which she applied to her collection, and which enabled her to figure out how to create functionalities that would suit her pieces.

Bedarida notes: "At the core of the majority of Marina's bracelets and collars was a supple steel spring. This allowed the jewel to remain exactly where it was intended on the wearer's neck or wrist, while not being overly constrictive. Her approach to jewellery was always that of a highly creative engineer; she was fascinated by the technical challenges which she then worked into the beautiful pieces that she produced." Bedarida adds: "Marina believed that high on the neck was the most attractive place for a jewel

to be worn, and so devoted herself to the creation of an extraordinary array of collars." These were a major part of her collection in the early 1980s. She enclosed the spring wire in precious metal, a device which allowed her choker necklaces to fit snugly and comfortably embrace the neck, moving with the women wearing them. The spring also allowed them to be put on and removed effortlessly.

She designed her own Marina B gemstone cut, which was between a triangle and pear-shape, as well as creating diamond jewels for daywear. She pushed the envelope to create jewellery that was both, graphic and bold, yet feminine and luxurious. Her designs were of the moment – powerful, uncompromising and unapologetic. Much like the women for whom she was designing, she had to stake her own claim in a predominately man's world, and she did it with grace, and innovative and imaginative flair. Marina B was first sold in the late 1990s, along with an archive containing over 12,000 design renderings. In 2017, after a succession of owners, Marina B came under the stewardship of Guy Bedarida, whose prior roles included Head Designer and Creative Director at John Hardy, and Head Designer of Van Cleef & Arpels USA, where

> 'Triangles' gold parure of sprung expandable choker, expandable bangle and ear clips, Marina B, 1980s. © Sotheby's

V Set of three diamond 'Onda' necklaces, Marina B, circa 1980. © Sotheby's

he created exclusive one-of-a-kind jewels for celebrities. Earlier in his career, he also worked at Place Vendôme in Paris creating high jewellery for the House of Boucheron. Since taking over the brand, Bedarida has brought back Marina B classics and created collections that are infused with the DNA of the brand.

Many of the designers of the early '80s pieces can be found through dealers or at auction houses. They still evoke the same power and confidence and can be worn for multiple occasions. They have also influenced trends in jewellery in recent years, as women look to make a bolder statement with their jewellery.

Rocks on the Block
Buying at Auction

< A 1935 Cartier bracelet displayed in front of a photograph of Wallis, The Duchess of Windsor for the auction of 20 pieces from her jewellery collection at Sotheby's, London, 23 September, 2010. The jewels were among the 250-plus pieces featured in the original 1983 sale. © Photo by Peter Macdiarmid/Getty Images

Before jewellery auctions were bustling with multiple telephone specialists, computers relaying internet bids, and rooms filled with well-suited men looking for engagement rings and couture-clad women looking for rare and unusual pieces, there was a time when only a secret society of dealers, die-hard collectors and celebrities were the predominant buyers at auction.

However, since around 1987, the auction houses have become a prevalent shopping venue for antique, vintage and modern jewellery for the public. The intimidation element that surrounded auctions stopped being a factor in the late '80s. Everyone from novice collectors

to self-purchasing women began to look to auction houses for their jewellery purchases. Ward Landrigan, owner of Verdura and Belperron, headed the Sotheby's New York Jewelry Department from 1965 to 1973 and remembers it well: "The Jewels of the Duchess of Windsor sale in 1987, visited by more than 2,500 people, and the 1996 sale of the jewels from the estate of Jacqueline Kennedy Onassis, visited by more than 12,000, were the main turning points in public interest."

David Bennett and Daniela Mascetti, co-authors of the world-renowned book *Understanding Jewellery* (ACC Art Books) and co-creators and experts of the Understanding Jewellery website, concur with Landrigan. The duo spent a combined total of 80 years at Sotheby's in different capacities: Bennett joined the company in 1978 and became Worldwide Chairman of the Jewellery Division, a position he held until 2020, and Mascetti, who joined the company in 1980, became the European Chairman of the Jewellery division until 2020.

Bennett explains: "The Duchess of Windsor sale was the turning point in demystifying how the public viewed auctions. I remember the queue that

∨ Bulgari *en tremblant* floral brooch, white and coloured diamonds set in platinum, 1959. The piece sold for $1,142,500 at the Christie's 2011 'The Collection of Elizabeth Taylor: The Legendary Jewels' sale. © Bulgari Heritage Collection. Photo: Barrella – Studio Orizzonte Gallery

built up outside the preview. It was unprecedented." Mascetti jumps in: "The Duchess of Windsor sale received so much advanced worldwide press coverage, which resulted in people coming from near and far to attend the previews."

Bennett continues: "Up until then, the general public had no idea that you can come in, touch and try on the jewellery and, particularly for the celebrity sales, that was a big draw. We saw it happen again with the Sotheby's sale of The Ava Gardner Collection in 1989 and 1990, and Christie's 2011 The Collection of Elizabeth Taylor: The Legendary Jewels, to name just a few more. The majority of

the public did not start to purchase at the 1987 Windsor sale, but their interest was piqued and soon after we saw the auctions open up more and more throughout the '90s and well into today."

Since then, there have been cultural and social influences affecting the growth of jewellery being bought at auction.

For this book's purposes, we will concentrate on the growth of vintage jewellery sales. Women from all over the globe began to take their cue from celebrities, who were no longer opting only for mega-watt diamonds for red carpet events, but choosing to wear more individual, unusual antique and vintage pieces. These A-listers are representative of the overall shift in the lifestyles of

modern women desiring more choice. They are in the market for unique and rare pieces – they don't want to see themselves coming and going – and they have found that the auction sales provide both signed and unsigned jewellery from different periods that they might not be able to find anywhere else.

Sotheby's and Christie's, as well as some of the smaller auction houses such as Phillips, Bonhams and Skinners in Boston, have captured the public's attention with a mix of savvy marketing, special events and lavish presale cocktail and dinner parties, and during the past 10 years, the internet.

"Back in the 1980s we started providing condition reports and offered certificates where we could find them. As time went on, we also made the catalogues more reader friendly and retail-oriented, adding a glossary of jewellery terminology, as well as stories about the estates and the design houses in the sale," says Mascetti. She continues: "All of this was very useful in helping the public to understand what they would be buying."

The previews also became more like a high-end retail shop, replete with velvet neck forms, display towers and cases, mirrors and flattering lighting. Pieces are merchandised by colour, designers/Houses, time period, provenance and/or theme, and

jewellery specialists are on hand to answer questions that clients and perspective customers might have. This has created a more accessible, user-friendly atmosphere for the public to come in, try on, get condition reports and really understand what they might want to bid on.

Frank Everett, Sotheby's Vice Chairman for Jewelry Americas, reports: "Over the past 10 or so years, the internet has really taken over. Instagram is perfect for jewellery as you can see pieces up close and in more detail than in the catalogues. On my feed I can show the back, front and intricate elements of a piece. On IG, those interested can get more detail of a piece than sitting across from a woman at lunch. These posts, plus other social media content and online sales are attracting a whole new generation of customers under 40 who are looking to buy."

He continues: "Although the previews are still a wonderful way to see the jewellery in person, try on and feel the pieces, online bidding has grown as a way to peer into the auction world at home, if they want to talk to specialists and get photos and bid in their pyjamas. It really has taken different routes." Everett has his own YouTube channel and produces approximately 10–12 videos per year about specific legendary sales which sometimes consist of

interviews with jewellery historians. One that he mentions is Elsa Peretti's 50th anniversary with Tiffany & Co., which definitely warranted a video.

The cyclical nature of jewellery has affected what dealers are buying and selling, what contemporary designers are inspired by, and what the auction houses are taking in and featuring in their sales. "Pieces that are coming up at auction are in keeping with the trends we have been seeing on the international runways," Everett notes, explaining: "Our auctions are including a lot more great collections of '70s/'80s jewellery, which is on target with these decades that are influencing fashion. This is also attracting the attention of younger and newer customers."

The big question when buying vintage jewellery at auction is whether to purchase signed or unsigned pieces. I asked some of the experts this question and they provided some insider knowledge for you to consider when thinking about bidding at auction.

Everett explains that there are advantages to buying both. "If you are a consummate collector of a certain time period or of certain designers/

Houses' collection, then signed pieces representative of that decade will hold their value and most often appreciate with time."

Mascetti agrees: "You would want signed pieces if you are building a collection. But if you are looking for beautiful pieces that are well made and reflect the period you are interested in, if all is right with the condition report, and if you have a set price, then there is nothing wrong with purchasing a high quality jewel that doesn't have a signature. You also need to consider what you can afford."

Both agree that during the 20th century, many jewels in Paris were made by the same workshops as the

< Van Cleef & Arpels gold and diamond demi-parure, circa 1975. The pendant is detachable and the sautoir can be taken apart to be worn as six bracelets. Each piece is signed and the lot was sold complete with two Van Cleef & Arpels letters of authenticity. © Sotheby's

established companies such as Cartier, Van Cleef & Arpels and Boucheron. "Therefore, you will be getting a piece that is in keeping with the superb quality and you will be paying much less for a style that has all the appropriate elements of the time," says Mascetti.

Everett adds: "Every great period of design during the 20th century followed certain popular styles. Personally, I am in the market for an Art Deco double clip brooch and I am quite certain that I can find an unsigned one in the same feeling with unparalleled craftsmanship for a third of the price that a Cartier or Tiffany & Co. would go for. The choice is yours and it's very dependent on what you can afford and what type of collector you are."

Additional Important Tips for Buying at Auction

Do your research

David Bennett: "If you are interested in purchasing a piece or pieces at auction, you should obtain all the knowledge you can get your hands on. Learn about the period in which the piece was made, read up on the styles of that period. Educate yourself about the market and prior auctions that have included pieces similar to those you are interested in.

See what the estimates were and then what the pieces sold for. Learn about the provenance of the pieces: are they from an important estate, a family, or a trade dealer. Where the jewellery comes from will affect the price. I don't think you can be over prepared, particularly if you are a first time buyer or relatively new at buying at auction."

Everett says: "Do your homework and really understand what is in the condition report and what it means to you. Look for whether or not there are indications of repairs, gemstone replacements and indications that a diamond is a simulant. There are also times when a ring has been resized and, unfortunately, the maker's mark has been cut off. If it comes from a family estate, they share the stories with us, which we can then share with a prospective client. Therefore, make sure to partner with a specialist who will be able to tell you everything they know."

Enlist an expert

Bennett recommends enlisting an outside expert to help you go through all the processes and to help guide you along to understand more about the pieces you are interested in, as well as the condition reports. "They can also aid you in deciding what your cut-off point should be, and even bid, based on the highest you can go, so your emotions don't take over while you are in the thick of it all."

Buy what makes your heart skip a beat

Both Everett and Mascetti are proponents of 'buy what you love'. Everett says: "You should always remember that pieces which come up at auction are often rare and you might never see them again. Therefore, if you are passionate about a jewel, you should think twice before letting it go. You might go a bit beyond your budget for this piece but it will be well worth it in the end."

Mascetti says: "If it goes with your style and personality, and you think that it will become an everyday jewel that you will cherish and get plenty of wear out of, then it is a jewel worth bidding on."

Ask questions

Bennett suggests asking these questions: "Are there comparable pieces the specialist can show you? What similar pieces have sold in the past three years and for how much?" He adds: "Never feel like you are asking too many questions. That is what the specialists are there for and to work with you on obtaining the information you need and then taking you through the sale."

Create your cut-off point

All experts agree: stick to your cut-off point; and know the commissions and tax that will be added to your item before you bid on it, then add that all up to create your cut-off point. "Adrenaline is pumping and in the heat of the moment you could get carried away," says Mascetti, "but you need to keep a clear head."

And as Everett states simply: "Don't chase something beyond your budget."

Understand the bidding process

Unlike luxury retail shops where you can plunk down your credit card and guarantee that you will leave with your purchase in tow, at auctions, private bidders sit in the auction hall with a numbered paddle or are bidding online and when their lot comes up, they can either score the piece or bid it farewell. Try not to get swept away by the process and get into a bidding war, which drives the price way up, past the estimate or even what the piece is worth. Everett says: "There are two strategies to take: start bidding from the beginning to let other bidders know you want it, but still keep a level head while doing this and don't try to outbid someone to prove a point." He continues: "The other way is to wait until all the interested parties have made bids and to come in later and place your bids then. There is never a guarantee that someone won't swoop in and make the final bid and win the piece but it's a risk you take while purchasing at auction."

When you have won the piece

You should also know about the return policy – i.e., there isn't one. When the

auctioneer says "Sold!" the piece is yours. Customers cannot return or exchange the jewellery once they've purchased it, nor can they bring it in for repairs or cleaning. The occasion that a customer can return a piece is if the condition report is wrong; for example, if it was listed as 1890 but it is really from 1950, or if they don't reveal certain alterations to the jewel, like a shank that is not original to a rare antique ring.

Finally, are they true bargains when you shop at auction? In today's market, if you are going after the unsigned pieces, you have more of a shot at getting a great price. It isn't like the old days, or this story that Ward Landrigan recalls: "One of the best deals I ever got was at an auction of Clare Boothe Luce's jewellery.

She had this tragedy-comedy mask of emeralds and pearls and no one knew what it was. It had been commissioned by Jock Whitney and his wife Betsey Cushing to present to her as the 'Tony' for her play *The Women*. She'd said she wanted an award she could wear. I knew all about this, and I managed to get it at a very, very good price. Also, prior to purchasing Verdura and Belperron, I knew the pieces quite well. Once in a while, there would be an unsigned Verdura piece and a piece that was recognisable to me as Belperron, and I'd get a good deal."

In today's market, buying vintage jewellery at auction is more about choice, rarity, building a strong collection, finding beautiful work and craftsmanship, and the thrill of owning a part of history.

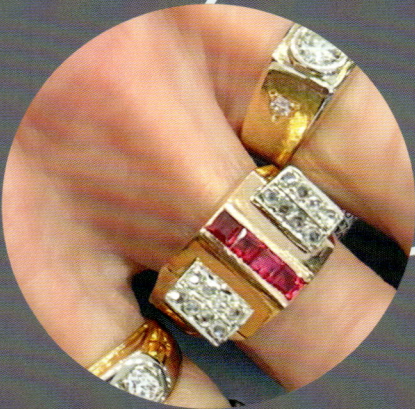

Wear and Tear
Wearing and Caring
for your Jewellery

Mixmaster – Jewellery Combinations From Different Eras

Styling vintage jewellery is instinctual, visual and, when you throw out all the rules, opens up freedom to a wealth of possibilities. Unless you are the type of collector who amasses jewels as a study in history, you will want to curate a collection that you can wear. As contemporary collectors who have a preference for vintage jewellery, we want to marry the past with the present, and have an eclectic, progressive approach when styling our unique pieces.

For this chapter, Frank Everett, Vice Chairman of Sotheby's Jewelry Americas, and Rebecca Selva, Chief Creative Officer for NYC's Fred Leighton, as well as yours truly, provide tips and suggestions on how to mix different decades in sometimes unexpected or unconventional ways that show these styles in a brand new light.

Everett explains: "It's personal, based on your individual taste and lifestyle. But there is also a fashion element to mixing different decades, it is art – with a small 'a' – as these pieces also have to be worn by a person with an outfit." With this being said, he continues: "I believe clothes should be a backdrop, allowing the jewellery to create the style statement."

He believes that the wrist is a great place to layer looks from different time periods, and mentions combining Art

Deco diamond flexible bracelets with one or two Cartier 'Love' bracelets and a retro '40s gold link chain.

I happen to agree, as that is exactly what is on my wrist as I write. I have also mixed these same pieces with contemporary, independent-designer, thinner bracelets, with and without diamonds, gemstones or 'mantra' words spelled out around the wrist, as well as a Victorian engraved floral nail bracelet.

Layered necklaces in graduated combinations has been *the* big trend on social media, both on the street and on the red carpet. You can start with an early '80s gold choker and wear it with a 1950s diamond necklace, a '70s astrological pendant with hardstone inlay for a pop of colour by Van Cleef & Arpels, and then maybe a strand of Elsa Peretti for Tiffany & Co. 'Diamonds by the Yard' in a longer length from the '70s or '80s. This mixes metals, diamonds and coloured stones.

Everett suggests trying "one of Marina B's famous spring chokers sprinkled with

styles have launched numerous trends and been huge hits on the red carpet with A-list celebrities. She advises: "Certain pieces of jewellery, no matter what time period, speak to each other – the textures, finishes and styles can work together aesthetically." She is also of the mind that mixing up vintage, antique and modern gives all of the jewellery a current feeling and allows women to get creative and wear their pieces more often.

Not everything will work at first. There will be trial and error. But isn't that the fun of it –to play and see what might look good together while at an auction preview, a dealer's or in a shop? Bring in the pieces you own and try them on with those you are attracted to and see what fits together and works best for you.

Cleaning and Care

Cleaning vintage jewellery is yet another aspect of collecting that you need to think about. Here are a few tips on the best way to do it yourself, and when you should take a piece to a jeweller.

When it comes to gold or silver vintage jewellery of any era, <u>never use chemicals</u>. Take a gentle polishing cloth and it will remove the silver tarnish and brighten up the gold.

If it is all gold, you can take a bowl with warm, soapy water and put the piece in there to loosen any dirt or buildup of

diamonds from the 1980s with one of Belperron's famous semi-precious cuffs set with a precious stone." He also sees 1930s Art Deco styles in combination with a contemporary Bulgari sapphire and diamond necklace. His advice is to "be bold and try different things".

Chief Creative Officer for Fred Leighton in New York, Rebecca Selva's uncanny instincts and visionary approach led her to curating and styling different time periods in jewellery for the past 20-odd years. She explains: "I see pieces in a completely different way, in that they don't need to be worn as originally intended." Selva's reworkings of these moisturisers or fragrances. Let it soak and then rinse and wipe with a soft cloth.

To clean jewellery with diamonds, sapphires and rubies (or any gemstones except pearls, emeralds or opals), use a soft toothbrush and some gentle washing-up liquid and water, and clean the stones if they're set in gold. Diamonds set in later Art Deco pieces onward can be easily cared for with the soap-water-toothbrush trick or a little window or glass cleaner, depending on the design around the piece. In pieces other than platinum, you want to make sure the vintage patina isn't damaged by cleaning. If you have any questions, take it to a professional jeweller to clean.

But pearl, opal and emerald pieces need a special type of cleaning that you should not attempt at home. They should be taken to a professional jeweller to clean.

Make sure to check all of the stones on all categories of jewellery from all periods before you wear the piece for the first time to ensure that none are loose in their settings and that no prongs are missing.

If you find you are wearing certain pieces regularly, then have them checked once every six months. The good news is that there are lapidaries that can cut

small stones to replace those that have fallen out, and this will not compromise the character or value of the piece.

Storing Your Jewels

Make sure that all jewellery is separated as this will keep chains from tangling and stones from scratching. You can keep them in separate compartments of a jewellery storage unit or lovely jewellery boxes they have on the market today. You can also store pieces in separate small zip-lock bags, which will keep them from scratching up against one another. There are numerous types of storage ideas found on the internet. One of my favourites is a jewellery binder that has separate sections like a photo album but is see-through. This also comes with substantial zip-lock bags of different sizes, which you slip into the sleeves of the binder and it saves a lot of space.

A wonderful way of storing the jewellery you wear in your daily rotation, but take off to sleep, is in jewellery trinket trays. These are often designed to be as decorative as the jewellery these trays are holding; there are different sizes for rings, bracelets, necklaces, charms and any other pieces you wear regularly. And they provide an easy way to find pieces you want to put on, and get out of the house quickly. They also make lovely ways of displaying your jewellery, like miniature works of art.

Building Blocks
How to Buy Vintage Jewellery

Shopping for vintage jewellery can transport you to a different time and place. It can lead to you wanting to know more about the lives of people who owned the pieces that caught your eye and touched your soul. If you are a new vintage jewellery enthusiast, it can also be challenging to discover which decade you favour. You might also question whether you are paying a price that's a fair reflection of the age, provenance and condition of a piece. At times it can be overwhelming, at other times exhilarating. This chapter will provide a handy guide, offering a range of tools that uncover the mystery of how to purchase vintage jewellery.

There is always something new you can learn that will help you develop a connoisseur's eye, whether you are a novice or a consummate collector. I have been collecting and writing about jewellery for 25 years, and I regularly discover something that I haven't learned, read or seen before. It always feels like a treasure hunt. And, for me, the thrill of the search is like a shot of adrenaline. I learned how to barter, bargain and sometimes beg, and I made mistakes along the way – which, as any collector and even the most seasoned of dealers will tell you, is unavoidable.

But the desire for one-of-a-kind jewels and pieces with history has created a new generation of vintage jewellery collectors.

So, how do you know what is authentic? Who do you go to? Where do you buy it from? Pre-internet, when I first started collecting, there were no search engines and we had to trek around on foot, talk to dealers, and read books and old magazines at libraries to find answers to our queries. I think that exploring different ways of finding and gaining knowledge is all important when you are starting to collect. I'm certainly thankful for the authoritative research that is provided on the internet, but nothing beats meeting face-to-face with those who share the same passion as you, seeing their merchandise in person, and gaining knowledge from trustworthy dealers while spending time with them. It's crucial to go into collecting jewellery with an openness to learning, you can gain an education while also having a whole lot of fun.

No one can teach you everything. Like any new hobby – or profession – there's a lot of trial and error at the beginning, but you can begin to gain an understanding by being around, seeing and feeling the jewellery. And there are definitely some helpful tips on how to shop for vintage jewellery for both novice and seasoned collectors. To pack all of this information into one chapter in a book is not possible, but I hope to share enough to get you started, to give you some basic knowledge and hopefully lead you to meet some wonderful and trustworthy dealers.

When you begin collecting, you may well be attracted to pieces that, in a few years, you trade up when you've learnt more about what's rare and interesting, or as your style changes. But while this is happening, you are still gaining knowledge firsthand, teaching yourself how to bargain and barter, and how to listen to your instincts, while meeting honourable dealers – those who are generous with their advice, just like all those who have contributed to the preceding chapters in this book. You will make your fair share of mistakes and discover your fair share of rare finds, just as I have done. Most importantly, you will find the styles, categories and time periods to which you are most drawn.

Starting Out

It can be intimidating when you launch into the world of vintage jewellery, but here are some handy tips:

Tip 1: Identify the decade (or decades) to which you are attracted

You can discover this by browsing shops and researching time periods in books, museum exhibits, auction catalogues and online sites. Also, it is important to look at examples of the most popular pieces and prevalent details from each era and get familiar with them.

Tip 2: Ask questions

If the dealer or shop owner is honest, trustworthy and passionate about what they do, they will be happy to talk to you about whether a piece is in its original condition or has been modified or 'reproduced', or if stones have been changed, and provide as much information as possible. Authentic original pieces in excellent condition appreciate with time, and all of the aforementioned benchmarks will affect the value of the piece.

Tip 3: How to buy signed pieces

Lee Siegelson reports: "When buying signed jewellery, an experienced and reputable dealer is absolutely essential. This field is filled with nuances that even a knowledgeable collector might miss, leading to serious risks of misattribution, overpaying, or even purchasing inauthentic pieces. Only a dealer with expertise and an established reputation can reliably navigate the complexities of signatures, craftsmanship, and provenance. Without this level of experience, a buyer is almost guaranteed to encounter pitfalls that can devalue or compromise the piece's legacy. Simply put, expert guidance is critical to making a secure, worthwhile acquisition."

Adam Patrick says: "When looking for signed pieces, you really want to be drawn by the design of the piece itself; even if the piece is signed, it should preferably be a one-off piece, which will keep its value far more than signed pieces that have been produced on a much larger scale. Finally, look at the quality and materials; generally, the more expensive or rare the materials, the better the piece."

Tip 4: Consider how often you can wear the piece

Think about your lifestyle and the type of piece you want to buy. If you are active and you want to wear the jewellery every day, ask if the piece can handle this type of wear.

Tip 5: Set your budget before you shop

You should understand that signed pieces are going to go for a much higher price than unsigned pieces from any of the decades of the 20th century. Again, this is

the time to do research: shop around and compare similar items from the same time period. If you are working with a dealer at a show or fair, you can ask for what's known as a 'dealer's price' – generally 10 or 20 percent off the ticket price.

Tip 6: Research dealers and seek out relationships

If you are looking for something specific, it is a good idea to research which dealers specialise in the time period that the piece was made, or its country of origin – ideally both. The importance of building relationships with retailers and dealers should not be underestimated. If you are a repeat customer, they will appreciate your loyalty and offer the same back, aiding you in your searches for desired pieces.

Tip 7: Wear, don't save your jewels

My advice to friends when they ask (or sometimes I give it unsolicited…) is not to buy jewellery to 'save' for a special occasion. Invest in 'wear now' – unless you plan on having a shop or a museum showing of your own.

Tip 8: Read as much as you can

There are so many great books out there about collecting vintage jewellery and also about the renowned Houses that are mentioned in this book. I would stay away from price guides, as price points change with supply and demand so these types of books struggle to remain current.

Tip 9: If it's too good to be true, then it is

If an Art Deco piece feels too crisp (as if it were recently cast, or the diamonds are too perfect) you should be suspicious. There are many forgeries out there.

One way to help ensure that what you are getting is genuine when you purchase a piece, is to ask for a receipt with as much information as possible on it – including a full visual description with a photo and details about age, time period, provenance, maker's marks and price. If you find out you bought something that isn't what it was claimed to be, you should be able to return it, if you have proof that it has been misrepresented to you.

Buying at Fairs and Markets

Many dealers and store owners participate in large trade fairs or antique/vintage markets, so they're a great opportunity to see a wide range of pieces in one place. Here, our experts share some insider tips on shopping the shows.

"Get an advanced copy of the exhibitor list and floorplan. If you know any of the dealers, this will help you to plan out your route." Diane Richardson, The Gold Hatpin

"Before going, start to follow different dealers who are featured in the show catalogue on Instagram to see what they have to say, and go to their website, too, so you already know about their approach and specialisations when you meet them in person at their booth." Dana Kiyomura, Keyamour

"At the various antique/vintage shows, there is traditionally a series of educational lectures before the show opens or while the show is going on. Check these out and see which pertain to you and what you want to learn. This will be beneficial and give you a crash course in the jewellery that you'll be seeing on the show floor." Simon Teakle, Simon Teakle in Greenwich Connecticut.

"Starter collectors might want to visit dealers who carry pieces from a diverse range of vintage decades to learn more about what they are looking at. Don't be afraid to ask to try on pieces to get the feel of them. If the dealer brushes you off, then you might want to move on to someone else. You should look for the

dealers and shops who will be happy to talk to you about all aspects of the pieces they know and help you understand if it's right for you." Sandra Cronan, Sandra Cronan Ltd

"Figure out if you are looking for something in particular or you are looking around with no other goal than to be delighted and inspired by the beautiful and rare merchandise you will encounter. If you're shopping with a purpose, be goal-oriented and walk the aisles of shows or markets in an orderly fashion, stopping at the booths of dealers who might have what you're looking for (based on your prior research or information in the catalogue). If an exhibitor doesn't have the sort of stock you're after, you can ask for them to suggest someone who might. Many dealers are happy to help a customer find what they're looking for, even if it's not in their own booth or shop." Diane Richardson, The Gold Hatpin

"If you are attracted to a piece and you want to know more, ask the dealer to talk about it. Most dealers enjoy discussing their merchandise and are eager to convey their enthusiasm for their pieces in the hope of finding kindred souls who also love what they themselves find intriguing. You may begin a new collection this way or discover something that you didn't know you needed, or at least pick up some new bit of information." Diane Richardson, The Gold Hatpin

"If it's your first time at a show and you are interested in purchasing, you should take a friend who is more knowledgeable or hire a consultant for a couple of hours. Sometimes dealers are working with multiple customers at once and, although they will try to be helpful, it becomes difficult for them to talk to different people at the same time. If you are serious about buying a piece that might be out of your comfort zone, you could use support in deciphering what is authentic, whether the pricing is about right, what might be reproduced or altered. If you don't have a friend or the resources to hire someone, then take the time to research as much as you can on the internet that evening, and if you still want the piece, go back the next morning – the dealer may even agree to set it aside for you overnight." Elizabeth Doyle, Doyle & Doyle

"Take notes of who has what at what

price. Ask for a business card with the booth number on it so you can return later if you're not ready to make a decision on the spot. But be prepared for disappointment if you leave the booth without your treasure and someone else snaps it up before you return. Remember that if you feel confident with the dealer, the best time to buy a vintage piece is when you see it. If it's gone, something similar may not reappear anytime soon." Diane Richardson, The Gold Hatpin

"Ask if the dealer has a better price. This is expected at a show, fair or market, so never be apprehensive about asking. The dealer will tell you if they can come down or not and will be more surprised if you don't pop that question." Sandra Cronan, Sandra Cronan Ltd

"Take a break now and then. Grab a snack, stay hydrated, wear comfortable shoes, stop for lunch so you can sit down and refuel. You'll make better decisions if you're hydrated, fed, and refreshed. That will make sure you're ready to go treasure-hunting again!" Diane Richardson, The Gold Hatpin

Repairs and Reproductions

Here are some things to consider when determining both if the piece you covet is in its original condition, and how much you care about any aspects of the piece that may seem problematic. It might also apply when deciding what sort of repairs you may want to undertake, and which ones are acceptable should you ever want to resell a piece.

You should try and check whether the shank of a ring has been changed, and if so, when. Dealers might buy and sell rings that they believe to be of the period but which have undergone some minimal restoration.

How much a piece has been repaired is an important factor in making your purchasing decision. Too many repairs, and the piece will have lost much of its value. It also could fall apart. Consider how many gemstones have been replaced. If you spot any damage, research what can and can't be fixed and how these repairs might affect the value.

Only you know if you would have been happier to wait for a piece that is completely authentic. We all learn as we go, and the lessons we gather along the way turn us into more adept collectors.

Knowledge is important but purchasing jewellery you love should be a joyful experience. You can go slowly and build your collection gradually as you learn more and more about the pieces to which you are attracted and how they fit into your modern lifestyle. While you do, check into this chapter every now and then for a refresher – and have fun and go shopping!

Shopping Guide

< French Art Deco aquamarine and diamond ring in platinum, circa 1940.
V< René Boivin 'Hindu' emerald necklace in gold, circa 1940.
V> Suzanne Belperron Art Deco yellow diamond clip in gold and platinum.
All images courtesy of Pat Saling Jewelry Collection

DEALERS AND SHOPS

A La Vieille Russie
Manhattan, New York
alvr.com

"Our motto is 'Where the unusual is usual,'" says A La Vieille Russie's Gallery Director, Peter Schaffer. "We always try to open our clients' eyes to the art behind the jewellery and help them understand the true significance of a piece." A La Vieille Russie is a beloved New York City institution, which has called the city home since 1933, first at the Rockefeller Center and then at the Sherry-Netherland hotel, before moving to its current location just down the street at 745 Fifth Avenue. Founded in Kiev in 1851, the gallery, now run by the fifth generation, has maintained an impeccable reputation for scholarship and integrity.

ALVR has a rich and fascinating history of collecting, from being credited with introducing the work of the Russian court jeweller (and loyal client) Carl Fabergé to American audiences, to helping form major museum collections. The company has garnered international praise for its world-class collection of rare jewellery, which includes pieces dating from the 18th century through to the 1970s. Over the years, they have worked with some of the most stylish people from Hollywood,

royalty, business and politics, including Audrey Hepburn, Frank Sinatra, William Randolph Hearst, Salvador Dalí, Anna Pavlova, Jacqueline Kennedy Onassis, Marilyn Monroe, Oscar de la Renta and Gloria Vanderbilt. "What we love about our work is that we get to continue to devote ourselves to seek out pieces with intrinsic and alluring beauty, never buying a piece solely for the name," says Schaffer.

Circa 1700
Los Angeles, California
@circa1700

Susan Cohen of Circa 1700 is a multi-talented renaissance woman. She is a screenwriter, who started to collect antique jewellery from the Georgian and Victorian era, captivated by the meaning and messages behind the pieces. In 2007, her personal passion for this type of jewellery led her into a second career as an antique jewellery dealer, selling on different platforms and on social media. Inspired by the symbolism and sentiment of the antique pieces she collected, she eventually transitioned into creating her own limited-edition and one-of-a-kind pieces with a nod to the past. Over the last several years of hunting down and finding unique treasures, Cohen has become enchanted by the charms of the 1950s, astrological symbols

of the '50s – '70s, and anything and everything Aldo Cipullo designed in the 1970s. In between writing for TV and film and creating her own designs, she has found rare, signed pieces from Cartier, Van Cleef & Arpels and Bulgari, as well as other major Houses, from the mid- to later part of the 20th century. She loves the hunt and will set out to find her clients what their hearts desire through her network of vintage dealers and secret haunts, where she has found some of her most riveting pieces.

D&E Singer
New York, New York
@Abbott_and_Austin

Diana Singer is a longtime dealer and highly respected member of the jewellery industry, as well as the scion of a family business spanning three generations. After graduating magna cum laude with a double major in French and Political Science from NYU and receiving her GG degree from the GIA, she relocated to San Francisco to run a small but highly specialised antique jewellery boutique named Antoinette's. She felt her role there was less that of a jewellery salesperson and more of an adoption agency for jewels that needed a new home. Always a passionate advocate for women's roles in the industry, she was a founding member of the

Women's Jewelry Association and won the Retailer of the Year award in 1988. After five years on the West Coast, she moved back to New York City to learn the intricacies of the wholesale trade. She continues to work in the industry, both as a wholesaler and as CEO of the vintage jewellery company, Abbott & Austin.

Singer has always been fascinated by the history of jewellery and gemstones and is the current president of the American Society of Jewelry Historians. She has written numerous articles for scholarly journals and magazines on various jewellery-related subjects, and she taught jewellery-buying skills at the fondly remembered 'Jewelry Camp' of the 1990s. She has spoken professionally at Sotheby's, at the GIA Annual Symposium, and for various appraisers' associations. Says Singer: "Despite decades in the industry, my daily enthusiasm for antique and vintage jewellery design hasn't waned; I remain an unrepentant jewellery addict and look forward to new discoveries every day."

Keyamour
Manhattan, New York
keyamour.com

As an army brat, Dana Kiyomura had an unconventional upbringing. She travelled the world with her parents and was fortunate to see the art and culture of Europe and the Far East up close in the sparkle of her youth – which later fuelled her passion for world history.

She graduated with a Major in History but discovered her calling when an internship at Christie's auction house turned into a job opportunity in the jewellery department. "I was fascinated by the pace of the dealers and the values," says Kiyomura. "My curiosity was particularly piqued when similar items fetched disparate prices. Soon, an affinity for the quality, craftsmanship and design of jewellery ignited my passions." After Christie's, Kiyomura was hired as the Director of Acquisitions for Fred Leighton. According to her: "Buying and curating collections for what many considered the finest antique jewellery retailer in the world was an amazing learning experience. My affinity for jewellery evolved when I was able to acquire the pieces that I loved for the store."

In 2016, after six years at Fred Leighton, Kiyomura decided it was time for her to prioritise her own endeavours. Wanting a name that 'unlocked' beauty and nostalgia with sentiments of 'love', she didn't need to look further than her own surname for inspiration. 'Kiyomura' turned into 'Key and Amour', and therefore the name of her new company was clear: Keyamour. "Our focus is on antique and vintage jewellery that isn't stuffy looking, but rather is relevant in a modern context. The Keyamour collection blends fashion and style; old meets new, attracting a global clientele who are stylish and expressive."

Doyle & Doyle
Manhattan, New York
doyledoyle.com

Doyle & Doyle has kept savvy New Yorkers and fashion insiders intrigued, purchasing and coming back for more than 23 years. Sisters Elizabeth and Irene Pamela Doyle founded the business in 1998 and continue to run it today. Before opening a boutique, they built their jewellery collection for two years by selling wholesale, online and to private clients. In 2000, they opened their first bricks-and-mortar store on the Lower East Side of Manhattan. After 13 years in this location, they moved their business to a larger, more art-gallery-style shop in the Meatpacking District. The larger space allowed them to expand Doyle & Doyle's special events, including jewellery exhibitions, lectures and presentations for New York Fashion Week. In March 2020, when New York City went into lockdown due to the Covid-19 pandemic, the sisters decided to close the boutique and pivot to online sales and virtual appointments. Due to demand, they added limited in-person appointments as soon as it was safe. The website doyledoyle.com is home to the full jewellery collection, highlighting a cross-section of antique and vintage pieces.

The Doyle & Doyle collection is thoughtfully curated to include different materials and techniques, inspiring stylish new ways to wear jewellery. As Elizabeth Doyle says: "My goal is always to choose jewellery that's meant to be worn and enjoyed, precious and storied but not so fragile that it can't be your go-to piece. But they also need to be collectable, for those who are building or adding to their jewellery collections."

Elle W Collection
Manhattan, New York
ellew.com

"I started out with a small shop in Westport, Connecticut over 40 years ago," says Lorraine Wohl, owner of Elle W Collection, "and have been lured by the legend, the magic and the intricacies of antique and vintage jewellery ever since." She began with what she could afford and what was selling. Wohl eventually moved to San Francisco, where she opened a store on Fillmore Street in 1979, concentrating on Edwardian and Art Deco pieces, "which complemented the extraordinary vintage clothing worn by patrons of the San Francisco Ballet and Opera". Wohl continues to tell her story: "Then in 1987, I began a love affair with New York and Paris, opening several stores, one on the East Side of New York City and one in the Marais of Paris. My true passion lies in 20th-century French jewellery. Owning the shop and an apartment in Paris allowed Wohl to shop the flea markets and antique/vintage fairs and get to know a range of different dealers, as well as continue to train her eye and concentrate on what would sell back in New York. When Wohl styled herself, she

captured this mix of times so well in her personal collection that she would often sell pieces right off her own wrist or neck, though she held on to sentimental pieces or jewellery she knew she would never find anything like again.

Today, her focus has broadened into Retro and the mid-20th century. She closed her Paris shop in 2013 to open a larger gallery-style location at the New York Design Center in New York City. Though she sells online, her main business is with a loyal clientele she has developed over many years, and their children and grandchildren.

Fred Leighton
Manhattan, New York
fredleighton.com

The home of Fred Leighton on Madison Avenue is a jewellery box glistening with gems that have graced Hollywood's elite – a roster of clients that reads like a *Who's Who* of style-setting celebrities – and pedigree pieces from the 1700s through to the 1970s.

At the heart and soul of this illustrious, world-renowned shop are museum-quality examples of period jewellery, an exquisite mix from all centuries. But Fred Leighton has surprisingly humble origins, considering the lofty heights it has reached.

The man behind the legend was one Murray Mondschein, born in the Bronx, the son of a cab driver father and a homemaker mother. When he returned from the army in 1959, after a brief stint out

in California, he purchased a clothing store in Manhattan's West Village that specialised in imported Mexican crafts, jewellery and wedding dresses. Named 'Fred Leighton', it became the go-to shop for those looking for pieces that had a unique, romantic bohemian quality. When Mondschein took in a range of Victorian consignment pieces, he knew that he was on to something. From there, he began to transform the way New Yorkers viewed antique and vintage jewellery. He began buying pieces from different time periods and famous provenances, including The Duchess of Windsor, Diana Vreeland and Brigitte Bardot. In 1986, he legally changed his name to Fred Leighton and moved the shop to Madison Avenue.

Leighton is credited as a pioneer in the antique and vintage jewellery business. While others were breaking apart jewels for the diamonds and other gemstones, Leighton's uncanny ability to spot rarity and authenticity and the true value of pieces put an end to this shortsighted practice, elevating the appeal of antique/vintage jewellery and making it both desirable and collectable. "Mr. Leighton could see behind the gemstones into the heart and character of the jewellery, and he created a whole new way to view, wear and collect these transformative and historical pieces," says Rebecca Selva, Chief Creative Officer, who has been with the company since 1992. In 2006, Leighton sold his business to Ralph Esmerian, who put the company into bankruptcy in 2008.

The Kwiat family purchased the company in 2009 and once again elevated it to its rightful place as 'Jeweller to the Stars', under the tutelage of CEO Greg Kwiat and the imaginative styling of Rebecca Selva, who is a master at creating a modern-day presence around pieces from the past. Selva's collaboration with actresses dates back more than 20 years, to when Miuccia Prada, a Fred Leighton client herself, asked for an antique choker for Nicole Kidman's first appearance at the Academy Awards in 1996 to complement a Prada gown. Rebecca and the Fred Leighton team have worked with Kidman ever since, as well as other stars on the red carpet, including but not limited to Lupita Nyong'o, Charlize Theron, Meryl Streep, Natalie Portman and Jennifer Aniston.

The Gold Hatpin
Oak Park, Illinois
goldhatpin.com
What started as an afternoon with friends at an outdoor antique show while on vacation, transformed into an over 35-year career in the antique/vintage jewellery business. Diane Richardson opened her shop in downtown Oak Park, Illinois, in 1985, offering silver collectables, hatpins and Bakelite jewellery. But as she honed her eye

and her talent for scouting out affordable jewels, her focus changed to fine pieces, from the Victorian through to the 1960s. Her store is not only a stop for locals but also a tourist attraction for people interested in antique/vintage jewellery from around the country. She has built a fanbase of international clients by participating in all of the major antique jewellery shows throughout the USA. Richardson also sells on her own website and Instagram (@goldhatpin).

Kimberly Klosterman
Cincinnati Ohio and
Hudson, New York
kklostermanjewelry.com
Kimberly Klosterman was first introduced to 1960s and '70s artist jewellery in 1996. As a student at Sotheby's 'Understanding Jewellery' course in London, she was exposed to works by jewellers such as Andrew Grima, Gilbert Albert and Arthur King. She learned about the ground-breaking International Exhibition of Modern Jewellery 1890–1961 at Goldsmiths' Hall in 1961 and it became her obsession.

Research fuelled her fascination for the field, and Klosterman, a dealer/collector, turned more to education. She has written and lectured on the subject for multiple museum audiences as well as jewellery historians. In 2020, a show of her personal collection of jewels entitled 'The Jeweller's Art – Revolutionary Jewellery of the 1960s and 1970s' opened in Europe at DIVA Museum in

Antwerp. It then travelled to the Schmuckmuseum in Pforzheim, Germany. And, in the spring of 2021, it came home to the Cincinnati Art Museum, where, with the help of chief curator Cynthia Amnéus, it originated under the name of 'Simply Brilliant: Artist-Jewelers of the 1960s and 1970s'. An illustrated catalogue accompanied the exhibition, which also included scholarly essays, artist biographies and makers' marks.

Macklowe Gallery
Manhattan, New York
macklowegallery.com
Macklowe Gallery was founded in 1967 by Barbara and Lloyd Macklowe with $300 and a dream. After decorating their home with second-hand objects, they attended their first antiques show at Madison Square Garden and were struck by the beauty of Tiffany lamps, though at the time they could not afford the $500 price tags. They purchased their first Tiffany vase, with the dealer allowing them to pay in $5 instalments over several weeks. They started antiquing on weekends, and Barbara, a jewellery lover, suggested selling one case of jewellery at the next show. They embarked on trips to Paris and London to scout the best Art Nouveau, Victorian and Georgian pieces, and over the next 46 years they continued to create a legendary shop, becoming known as the 'premier dealers' of museum-quality, 20th-century decorative arts and the largest global home of authenticated

Tiffany lamps. The couple remained at the helm of the organisation until 2012 when they handed the shop down to the second generation: their son, Benjamin Macklowe, who became president of the company. The gallery is now under the full leadership of Benjamin and Hillary Macklowe. Benjamin Macklowe explains: "Over the years we have placed decorative works of art in major public, private and corporate clients' collections, including the Metropolitan Museum of Art, the Museum of Modern Art, Dallas Museum of Art and the Australian National Gallery, among others." Benjamin Macklowe gives regular lectures at Christie's and Sotheby's, and at appraisal industry events. Part of the sprawling 6,000-foot gallery's uniqueness is the ability of everyone who works there to educate and promote the next generation of collectors. From the 1980s on, the gallery has attracted an A-list clientele, including Barbra Streisand, Faye Dunaway, Rod Stewart, Whoopi Goldberg and Steve Jobs. Today, Macklowe Gallery has one of the most comprehensive and highly prized collections of Art Nouveau jewellery, particularly the work of Louis Comfort Tiffany, as well as a stunning selection of Retro mid-20th-century jewellery.

Pat Saling
Manhattan, New York
patsalingcollection.com
Pat Saling began her career decades ago with the legendary Fred Leighton, overseeing the sales of exceptional jewels and working one-on-one with a wide array of celebrity clientele and collectors. In 2002, she launched the Pat Saling Jewel Collection. Everything is chosen with a connoisseur's eye, and Saling offers a broad selection of awe-inspiring pieces from the 19th and 20th centuries. Her company is especially devoted to the French Art Deco era and features many original pieces by René Boivin and Suzanne Belperron.

Saling selects pieces for their creativity in design, superior workmanship and historical significance. Her knowledge and appreciation of timeless artistry and beauty are reflected in her fine selection of these masterful jewels. As she says: "My goal is to find jewellery from the past that continues to resonate aesthetically with contemporary fashion and culture." In 2017, Pat's son, Parker joined her to help manage the collection. Together, they are striving to broaden the company's range and further its unique vision.

Platt Boutique Jewelry
Los Angeles, California
plattboutiquejewelry.com
Sibling duo Larry and Natasha Plotitsa have jewellery in their genes: their heritage dates to the golden age of great Russian jewellers and artisans. Their family eventually emigrated to the USA and settled in Chicago. They learned part of the business from their father, a diamantaire who developed a thriving diamond business in custom engagement rings. But the siblings took a different route, purchasing jewellery from across the ages and presenting it so it feels relevant and modern against the backdrop of the current fashion moment. The focal point for the duo has been vintage engagement rings and unique antique jewellery, making them the darlings of a creative community in Hollywood and beyond that seeks one-of-a-kind pieces.

"We grew up in a home surrounded by antiques and history. Vintage jewellery has been a focal point of our business since day one," says Larry Plotitsa. Additionally, they possess the background and knowledge base to authenticate and appraise antique and vintage jewellery and signed pieces. They have grown from an antique/vintage engagement ring business to their current location – a sprawling shop that shares space with Larry's wife, Robyn, the curator of the designer women's vintage clothing boutique The Kit Vintage.

Rogue Vintage Jewels
New York, New York
@roguevintagejewels
Amie Park's passion for vintage fine jewellery began with her grandmother's cherished charm bracelet, brimming with sentimental significance. This early connection inspired a career with iconic brands, like

Cartier and Tiffany & Co., where she honed her expertise in exceptional craftsmanship and timeless design. This then led to her fascination with distinctive creations, including articulated and mechanical charms by Henry Dankner & Sons, which also produced for Tiffany & Co. and Van Cleef & Arpels.

Park began collecting for herself, which resulted in launching Rogue Vintage Jewels, specialising in remarkable 20th-century pieces with distinctive character. From signed treasures by Tiffany & Co. and Cartier to rare designs with rich histories, she curates collections that celebrate craftsmanship and storytelling, connecting clients to heirlooms that transcend time.

Sandra Cronan UK Ltd.
London, UK
sandracronan.com

Sandra Cronan learned about antique and vintage jewels and precious gemstones from her father. She eventually turned what had initially been a hobby into a business over 40 years ago. Cronan was one of the first female jewellers to be accepted into the British Antique Dealers Association (BADA). Cronan was joined by her business partner, Catherine Taylor, 20 years ago, and together they have built a reputation, finding and selling rare jewels from the 17th century through to the 20th century, which are chosen for their design aesthetic, distinctiveness of each period,

quality and wearability. As one of London's leading antique and vintage jewellery specialists, Cronan and Taylor not only continue to add to and sell an expertly curated range of jewellery, but they also seek out particular items based on client's desires.

Siegelson
Manhattan, New York
siegelson.com

Lee Siegelson, a third-generation gem and jewellery dealer, has bought and sold some of the greatest examples of jewellery for nearly a century. His gallery is globally renowned for offering extremely rare and collectible jewels. In the past decade, the company has loaned more than 100 works to more than 25 exhibitions and has sold 20 jewels to museum collections. His instincts are impeccable and he has a discerning eye for acquiring the unique and important creations throughout multiple time periods. His interest in fine objects is the opposite of the commercialism and mass production that he feels is "ever-present in the jewellery industry today". He explains: "I focus on pieces designed without compromise and with the utmost quality and beauty." He is often quoted in the press and has been hailed by *Vogue* Paris as 'New York's King of Jewelry'. He is quoted throughout this book on the Art Deco period, the women trailblazers of the 1930s and the legendary jewellery of the 1950s, as well as the

changing times of the 1960s and 1970s, providing examples and speaking about pieces that have passed through his hands.

Simon Teakle
Greenwich, Connecticut
simonteakle.com

Simon Teakle, owner of his namesake store and website, which opened in 2012, has a long history of examining rare pieces and educating customers on jewellery, following his 20-year stint running the Christie's New York department. Teakle is one of the go-to experts quoted by online magazines and print editors as his knowledge is broad and deep. When he was still working at Christie's, he began purchasing authentic and original pieces from many different time periods – pieces with history and provenance that would appreciate in value, but that women could wear easily in the modern day. He caters to private clients and sells globally from Asia to Europe. His well-appointed bricks-and-mortar store is an international stop for tourists in the beautiful town of Greenwich, where he features jewels ranging from Georgian through to the 1970s. His enthusiasm is boundless and he is often the first person to be found at the opening of antique fairs, seeking out pieces from international dealers that no one else has seen yet. When he speaks about jewellery, his excitement is infectious, and he has a remarkable ability to pair unique pieces with the collectors with whom they 'belong'. He specialises in both antique and vintage jewellery, and he continues to seek out pieces at varied price points so that novices can purchase from him as well as consummate collectors.

Wilson's Estate Jewelry
Philadelphia, Pennsylvania

wilsonsestatejewelry.com

Wilson's Estate Jewelry is a dedicated estate jeweller. The company opened its doors in early 2018, initially starting with a team of only two: the owner and founder Brad Wilson, and his highly skilled and enthusiastic dog, Gracie. Through the company's commitment to authentic and high-quality goods, it has become an industry leader in selling antique and vintage pieces. The team travels daily throughout the world in search of the finest 19th- and 20th-century pieces that have the distinctive qualities of workmanship, sophistication and rarity that Wilson says, "are not often found in modern pieces. This makes these pieces highly desirable to collectors and connoisseurs of jewellery. Because these items are not available in large quantities, they tend to retain their value." Brad Wilson's staff is now comprised of dedicated jewellery professionals aiming to connect their unique collection with the public. They can be found at many of the major antique/vintage shows throughout the USA.

OTHER DEALERS AND SHOPS

The following locations stock vintage jewellery from the periods featured in this book:

Aaron Faber Gallery – USA
Adin – Belgium
Berganza – UK
Eleuteri Italy – USA
FD Gallery – USA
G. Lindberg Jewels – USA
Gray & Davis –USA
Humphrey Butler – UK
Inez Stodel – Netherlands
Ishy Antiques – UK
Jacob & Co. – USA
Jewelrider – USA
Jewels by Grace – USA
Kentshire – USA
Lang Antiques – USA
Mary Ann-tiques – USA
Moira Fine Jewellery – UK
Spicer Warin – UK
S.J. Phillips – UK
Véronique Bamps – France
Wartski – UK

FAIRS & SHOWS

Las Vegas Antique Jewelry and Watch Show

lasvegasantiquejewelryand-watchshow.com

Where: Wynn Las Vegas, Nevada, USA

This is one of the few trade-only shows on the antique and vintage circuit, with dealers flying in from across the globe to exhibit and buy authentic period jewellery. While it does get busy, it is a bit less hectic without the consumer attendance, allowing participants to cover the show more efficiently. Its relocation last year to the Wynn – which is also home to the annual Couture jewellery show – is a welcome change, as it enables retailers who buy both estate and contemporary designs to shop one venue.

New York City Jewelry & Watch Show

nycjaws.com

Where: Metropolitan Pavilion, New York, USA

Small and easily navigable, this show is nonetheless brimming with leading estate jewellers and watch vendors. All of its approximately 100 exhibitors deal in jewellery, and you can make leisurely decisions as you peruse Georgian through modern designs, including many signed pieces. The fair is open to the public, so booths may get busy at times, but getting around is super easy in Manhattan, and the venue's central location means you can take in the city sights and return later. Just don't let your dream jewels slip away.

The NYC Jewelry & Object Show

www.nycjaos.com

Where: Metropolitan Pavilion, New York, USA

Following a successful inaugural edition in November 2023, the NYC Jewelry & Object Show expanded its lineup of antique and vintage jewellery exhibitors three-fold. It is held twice yearly in April and November and continues to grow and evolve, gaining more dealers who specialise in different time periods which span from Georgian through to the early 1980s. Attendees have access to these world-class dealers who are passionate about sharing their expertise. This show has a relaxed, intimate atmosphere, making it the destination for those who want to learn as much as possible about pieces that are of interest to them. It is produced by KIL Productions, established by Konstantinos Leoussis in 2023. The company is dedicated to creating accessible opportunities for vendors of all kinds, from all over the world, and curating a range of events spanning antique and vintage jewellery, watches, art objects, and contemporary jewellery design.

The Original Miami Beach Antique Show

originalmiamibeachantique-show.com

Where: Miami Beach Convention Center, Florida, USA

This huge multi-hall extravaganza celebrated its 60th anniversary in 2024. If you don't mind getting lost navigating the displays of home décor and vintage art, you'll find hundreds of world-renowned antique and vintage dealers who are happy to greet you.

They'll even tell you where else to look if they don't have the item you're seeking. The goods on offer range from accessibly priced Victorian jewellery to high-ticket signed vintage pieces. There is also an educational series each morning before the show opens, which covers a lot of informational ground.

TEFAF/ Maastricht and TEFAF/ New York

www.tefaf.com

Where: Maastricht Exhibition & Conference Centre (MECC Maastricht), The Netherlands Park Avenue Armory, New York, USA

Ten years ago, The European Fine Art Foundation (TEFAF) – whose long-running show in the Dutch city of Maastricht remains a prestigious hub for art, antiques and design – brought the fair to Manhattan. The organisers felt that New York, as one of the world's most vibrant art markets, provided an ideal setting for the fair outside of The Netherlands.

It is a beautiful show to walk; exhibitors have their own specialised gallery settings, and although the antique and vintage turnout is better in Maastricht, the New York edition is still lovely, well organised and inspirational.

The Treasure House Fair

treasurehousefair.com

Where: Royal Hospital Chelsea, London, UK

The Treasure House Fair features leading stores and dealers, including A La Vieille Russie, Sandra Cronan, Wartski, S.J. Phillips and more, with jewellery dating across multiple time periods. The fair, which was founded by Thomas Woodham-Smith and Harry Van der Hoorn, co-founders of the original Masterpiece fair in 2009, has created a showcase of enchanting art and design. It will enter a third edition in 2025 for one week during London's summer season. The exhibitors are all vetted by independent experts.

The Winter Show

thewintershow.org

Where: Park Avenue Armory, New York, USA

Celebrating 70-plus years as the longest-running art, antique and design fair in the USA, this show is truly like visiting a museum, with rare, authentic jewels spanning from antiquity to today. There are over 65 internationally renowned dealers in the fine and decorative arts. Special benefit events include the opening night party, which attracts collectors, celebrities and the press, and Young Collectors Night. All proceeds go to East Side House Settlement, which provides life-changing programs for communities in the Bronx and northern Manhattan.

Acknowledgements

There are so many people who helped with this book and without whom it couldn't have been done. First, my publisher James Smith, who believed in me for a fourth time and has always given me the creative freedom to test out new ways of introducing different styles in writing jewellery books. To all the team at ACC: Andrew Whitaker, the development editor, and the person who pushed me through the times when everyone I needed to speak to was on vacation and I never thought I would meet my deadline. His understanding and calming talks kept me going through the process. To Susannah Hecht, my editor, who I have been waiting to work with again since we worked on *If These Jewels Could Talk* ten years ago; I am so glad she was able to work with me and give me her insights and edits again.

To Alice Bowden, for her eagle-eyed proofreading. To Alison Hart, who has been there whenever I have a question or need to get in touch with someone – I don't think any of these books would have seen the light of day without your help. To the designer Craig Holden and art director Mariona Vilarós Capella, who both brought the book to life.

And to all of the dealers, heritage specialists at the established Houses, experts and expert friends who continued to go the extra mile for me in coordinating the proper photos and information, and who provided insight into each decade we worked on together. In particular, to Bruno Barba, Deputy Director Head of Luxury Communications at Sotheby's who helped me to fill in gaps with my multiple requests for photos and supplying them quickly every time I thought of a new missing illustration in the book. To Diana Singer, President of ASJH (American Society of Jewelry Historians) who has been a cheerleader for me from the beginning, and whose continued support has helped me in all of my endeavours. To Stacy McLaughlin, Michelle Peranteau and Debi Marx, three publicists who always ensured I received the information and photos I needed on time – I will be forever grateful for their professionalism and ongoing friendship.

I could not have worked with more knowledgeable people who gave freely their expertise and time.

And to all my friends in and outside of the jewellery world who supported in the past and continue to do so, through the process and believed that I could do it... again.

Bibliography

Amnéus, Cynthia. *Simply Brilliant: Artist-Jewelers of the 1960s and 1970s*. GILES, 2020.

Becker, Vivienne and Renato Cipullo. *Cipullo: Making Jewelry Modern*. Assouline, 2021.

Corbett, Patricia, Ward Landrigan, and Nico Landrigan. *Jewelry by Suzanne Belperron: My Style is My Signature*. Thames & Hudson, 2016.

Hargrove, Rosette. 'In Midst of Diamonds, She Wears One Jewel', *Binghamton Press*, 29 June 1951.

Horn, Cathy. 'Modern Before The World Was'. *The New York Times*, 20 December 2012.

Nemy, Enid. 'David Webb Heralds New Golden Age'. *The New York Times*, 28 June 1967.

Sandoz, Cecile. 'Jewels That Tell About Their Owners'. *The San Francisco Chronicle*, 1961.

Van Gelder, Lawrence. 'Designing With A Difference'. *The New York Times*, 1 January, 1984.

Warren, Virginia Lee, 'Jewelry That Has Sense of Movement'. *The New York Times*, 17 October 1970.

Cover images, clockwise from top left:
Original Aldo Cipullo 'Love' bracelet for Tiffany & Co., see p.9 (Courtesy of Platt Boutique Jewelry); Mauboussin 'Tutti Frutti' double clips, see p.14 (Courtesy of Sandra Cronan); Cherry brooch by Raymond Yard, see p.90 (Courtesy of A La Vieille Russie); 'Zebra' bracelet by David Webb, p.127 (Photograph courtesy of David Webb); Van Cleef & Arpels sapphire leaf clip, see p.8 (© Van Cleef & Arpels SA.); Bulgari 'Serpenti' watch, see p.112 (© Bulgari Heritage Collection. Photo: Barrella – Studio Orizzonte Gallery)

Frontispiece
Paul Flato floral brooch with pavé-set diamonds, New York, circa 1936. Courtesy of Lee Siegelson

---

ISBN: 978 1 78884 336 2

Editor: Susannah Hecht, Alice Bowden
Design concept: Louise Brody, louise brody design
Designer: Craig Holden, Mariona Vilarós Capella
Reprographics Manager: Corban Wilkin

EU GPSR Authorised Representative:
Easy Access System Europe Oü, 16879218
Address: Mustamäe tee 50, 10621 Tallinn, Estonia
Email: gpsr@easproject.com Tel: +358 40 500 3575

FSC
®
www.fsc.org
MIX
Paper | Supporting
responsible forestry
FSC® C019910

Printed in China by Artron Art Printing (HK) Ltd
for ACC Art Books Ltd., Woodbridge, Suffolk, England

www.accartbooks.com

**ACC
ART
BOOKS**